# Between Monks and Monkeys

# Between Monks and Monkeys

Gill Winter

## Cover photographs

Front: Monkey with prayer flags near McLeod Ganj
Back: Sunset over the Dhauladhar mountains, Dharamshala. In the
foreground are Himalayan pine and oak trees

## Drawings

iii. Monk at the Dalai Lama's teachings, Namgyal Monastery,
Dharamshala
v. Tibetan women at the Dalai Lama's teachings
vii. Woman on construction site, Central Tibetan Administration
viii. Woman in traditional chuba at the Dalai Lama's teachings
ix. Stray dog sleeping beside the Tibet Library. The triangular nick in its
ear shows it has been treated by Tibet Charity's vets
xi. Indian holy man sleeping by a vegetable stall, McLeod Ganj
130. Bronze sculpture, Harappa, Indus Valley, 2000 BC. Delhi Museum

First published 2011
Second edition 2014
Create Space edition 2014
Published by G Winter
833 Richmond Road, 3 RD New Plymouth, 4373 New Zealand
Email gillwinter.nz@gmail.com
This edition printed by Create Space

New Zealand ISBN 978-0-473-19522-9
E-book ISBN 978-0-473-20319-1
Create Space ISBN 9781500737351

**By the same author:**
*The Yeti in the Library* © G Winter, 2013
Paperback ISBN 978-0-473-23647-2
E-book ISBN 978-0-473-23646-5
Create Space edition ISBN 9781500908508

Website www.gillwinterbooks.com
Travel blog http://journals.worldnomads.com/flyingpiglet

## About the author

Gill Winter spent eleven years working as publicist and public programmes organiser at the Govett-Brewster Art Gallery, one of New Zealand's premier contemporary art museums. She left the art world in 1999 to create Flying Piglets, a touring agency for folk and blues musicians. During the next few years she also worked as marketing manager for the Lake Taupo and Taranaki Arts Festivals, helped on the family pig farm and was a regular volunteer for Trade Aid, New Zealand's largest Fair Trade organisation.

In 2009, she wound up Flying Piglets and completed a CELTA course in teaching English as a second language. In 2010, she answered an advertisement on the Jobs page of *Dave's ESL Café* website for volunteer teachers to work in Dharamshala, India.

She is married with two adult children and lives in Taranaki, New Zealand.

# Contents

# Dedication

This book is dedicated to Alex, Adrian and particularly Pete,
with my love and grateful thanks for your tolerance
and support during my various career changes.

In memory of Beryl Burnett, whose joie de vivre, open mind
and sense of adventure had a huge influence on me.

# Acknowledgements

Firstly I want to thank Tibet Charity. Their advertisement for volunteer teachers gave me the opportunity to travel to India and stay there for three fascinating months.

My lovely students made teaching in Dharamshala a real pleasure. I am also grateful to my fellow teachers for their friendship and for the experiences we shared together.

There were a number of people who generously gave me their time and assistance while I was writing this book. David Hill saw an early draft of the first chapter and gave me constructive feedback. Willow O'Shea read part of the manuscript and had some useful comments to offer. Special thanks to Antona Wagstaff for her patient and thoughtful editing.

I also made extensive use of PublishMe's website, a great resource with plenty of good advice for writers.

If you can, help others.
If you cannot do that,
at least do not harm them.

His Holiness the 14th Dalai Lama

# Introduction

In late 2010, I spent three months teaching English to adult students at Tibet Charity in Dharamshala, India. I wrote regular emails while I was there and also kept a diary. However, after I returned to New Zealand, I started thinking about all the things I *hadn't* written about. I wanted to capture the feeling of Dharamshala and understand more about why I found it such a special place.

This book represents my individual perspective on life in India, and I am solely responsible for any mistakes in translation or errors of interpretation.

In the interests of privacy, I have changed the names of everyone in the book, except for well-known figures like His Holiness the Dalai Lama, Jetsun Pema and the seventeenth Karmapa. I have also used the real names of people whose jobs take them into the public eye, such as Satender of Salaam Baalak Trust and Tashi of Sangye's Kitchen.

Dharamshala is a city on two levels, separated by 550 metres of mountainside. I have used 'Dharamshala' to refer to the city as a whole, and 'McLeod Ganj' or 'McLo' when talking about the upper town.

At the back of the book is a glossary of the foreign words and abbreviations used in the text.

If you want to know more about the work of organisations such as Tibet Charity, Salaam Baalak Trust or the Tibetan Children's Village, you can find their websites at the back of the book.

Tashi delek!

*Chapter One*

# *Delhi*

"So," said Nina the German Buddhist, "You're going on the night bus to Dharamshala. The Volvo bus?"

"I don't know," I said. "The hotel booked it for me. It cost five hundred rupees."

"Oh, the cheap bus. No aircon. Very cramped. You'll be sick on the hairpin bends. The Volvo bus is better, but that one is terrible. Everyone is sick."

*Great!* I thought. *I'm eating a big plate of momos and I'm going to lose it all on the bus tonight.* I could see myself emerging in Dharamshala, pale, clammy, clothes smelling of vomit. *Oh well*, I thought, *At least nobody's meeting me.*

Nina and I were sitting in the dimly lit restaurant of Wongdhen House hotel in the Tibetan enclave of Delhi. I had invited myself to her table - not something I would do at home, but here I was a stranger in a strange land and everything was possible. She had recommended the momos, a type of Tibetan dumpling, and honey lemon ginger tea, which was tangy and delicious.

"And what are you doing here in India?"

"I'm going to teach English to Tibetan refugees," I told her. "For three months, as a volunteer at Tibet Charity."

"What a good thing to do! Have you taught in many countries?"

"Actually," I confessed, "I only qualified last year. This is the first time I've done something like this. I'm very excited."

"But you've chosen a wonderful place! I've been there many times. Dharamshala is such a beautiful town, up in the mountains. You know that His Holiness the Dalai Lama lives there? And of course Tibetan Buddhism is so profound…"

1

And she launched into an enthusiastic account of her personal journey into Buddhism. She spoke about geshes, mantras, samsara, meditation …

A niggling little worm of doubt began to insinuate itself into my mind. *What the hell are you doing here?* it sneered. *What do* you *know about Buddhism or Tibetans? You think you can march in and teach them English? You ignorant, middle aged, middle class Kiwi!*

Virtually every moment of my first twenty-four hours in Delhi had been an education. The previous afternoon as my taxi pulled out of the airport carpark I had hardly known where to look first. Released from the sheltering cocoon of air travel, I suddenly felt a very long way from small, safe, regulated New Zealand.

An endless mass of cars, trucks and buses vied with one another for right of way. Puttering tuk tuks with *Sound horn! Keep distance!* painted on the back edged past bicycle rickshaws and cyclists on battered bikes, some with huge, crazily balanced loads. There were motorbikes ridden by helmeted men with bare-headed, elegant women in saris riding side saddle on the pillion. A cacophony of horns filled the air and a sickening smell of exhaust fumes wafted through the taxi.

In the shade of the dusty trees I saw the occasional charpoy on which a languid figure reclined. The sleeper always seemed to be a man. Women in bright saris were carrying heavily laden bowls of earth on their heads to construction sites beside the road. Armed soldiers lurked behind piles of sandbags at major intersections, while dogs and crows scavenged through piles of rubbish.

My taxi driver was a slender young man who looked about eighteen and clutched the wheel with ferocious intensity. His English was minimal but in any case he had no spare energy to waste on chatter, and we made the journey in total silence. He had been sent by my hotel to pick me up  -  for quite an exorbitant fee, I had originally thought - but the ordeal of driving in Delhi traffic was clearly so demanding that I decided to give him a generous tip at the end of the journey.

As we neared Majnu ka Tilla, the Tibetan settlement in Delhi, we passed a row of decrepit apartment houses whose surroundings were completely flooded with muddy rubbish-strewn water from the nearby Yamuna river. Several cars were submerged up to their bumpers.

At the edge of Majnu ka Tilla the driver poked the taxi's nose in among a huddle of similarly battered cars and rickshaws, locked the doors carefully and, carrying my bag on his shoulder, led me through a tangle of narrow alleyways to Wongdhen House. It had been recommended as clean, not unbearably noisy, and cheap for a Delhi hotel.

I settled into my basic but adequate room, managed to reduce the fan from a hurricane to a breeze and had a pretty good night's sleep.

Next morning I set out to let the family know I'd reached Delhi and was still alive and well. The hotel receptionist told me the local internet cafés were out of action because of the monsoon flooding. If I wanted to send an email, she said, I would need to take a rickshaw and the metro to somewhere called Rajiv Chowk.

"You are married, madam?" shouted the rickshaw driver, peddling furiously through the traffic. "Children? How many? I have four sons!"

I entered the metro station with some trepidation, remembering various miserable experiences on the dirty, smelly London Underground. It was a welcome surprise to find that although the train was jam-packed it was modern, clean and air conditioned. Upcoming stations were helpfully indicated on an electronic sign as well as by loudspeaker.

The air on the street at Rajiv Chowk was thick with exhaust fumes. The traffic barrelled endlessly past, five chaotic lanes deep. I could see an internet sign across the road but how on earth to reach it? Eventually I took myself in hand. A man in the crowd stepped out into the traffic and I lurked close beside him. In an erratic, heart-stopping series of moves, we made it safely across the street.

The internet café was small, hot and crowded with men. The keyboard was filthy, and the man beside me insisted without explanation on commandeering my computer to print a document. I sent my emails as quickly as possible, shadowed a young woman back across the street, found the metro station and retraced my steps to Majnu ka Tilla.

Back at Wongdhen House, I got ready to take the overnight bus to Dharamshala. The hotel receptionist had kindly booked my bus ticket for me, although whether she had done me any favours by booking me on the cheaper bus was still to be seen. Departure time was six o'clock, so I decided to have an early dinner in the hotel restaurant. It was there that I met Nina the German Buddhist.

Before we parted, Nina insisted on giving me a blister pack of four motion sickness pills.

"Take one after the first restaurant stop, before the hairpin bends."

I found a plastic bag in my luggage, stuffed it into the top of my daypack where I could whip it out in an emergency, and prepared for an uncomfortable night on the bus and the likely reappearance of the momos.

*Chapter Two*

# Twelve hours to Dharamshala

Two hours later we had left the straggling outskirts of Delhi behind and were well on our way to Dharamshala. The bus seemed to be in good condition and was only moderately uncomfortable. It was pretty crowded but I was fortunate to have an empty seat beside me.

The young Tibetan woman across the aisle gave me a beaming smile every time she caught my eye. The sari-clad Indian woman one seat back was gazing serenely out the window. In front of me, two young monks in maroon robes were plugged into Ipods. The only other European on the bus, a small dark haired woman, was muttering to herself as she scrabbled through her daypack.

Our first stop was a modern restaurant with clean squat toilets. The dark haired woman and I drifted together and ordered glasses of chai. She was English, on a two-year stay in India, and was thoroughly disgruntled at finding herself on this inferior bus. She had booked for the Volvo coach, she said, waving her receipt, and someone was going to have to answer for the mistake.

We made our way back to our bus just as a rather more upmarket tour coach drew into the carpark. *Panicker's Travel Ltd* was painted in big letters above the windscreen.

It was dusk as we drew out of the carpark and the night soon became very dark, apart from the occasional flash of oncoming headlights.

Some time later I became aware that we were climbing slowly and steeply and thought *These must be Nina's hairpin bends!* Most people seemed to be asleep. Nobody appeared likely to throw up. I'd forgotten to take Nina's sickness pill but my stomach seemed perfectly calm. What a relief!

A full moon was rising. I could just make out the silvery shapes of trees beside the road and an occasional glimpse out over the misty plain. Except for the muffled roar of the motor and the tinny chatter of someone's Ipod, the bus was silent.

About half an hour later, the monk in front of me opened the window, leaned out and discreetly - and rather neatly I thought - threw up into the night.

Our second stop was a ramshackle hut with a steaming kettle on the fire and small grubby glasses for chai. The young Tibetan woman and I groped our way with the aid of my torch to the 'toilet', a patch of damp dirt behind the hut. The surly tea man sold his well stewed chai at twice the price we'd paid on the plains. People sat hunched and silent over their glasses. It was 4 am.

The final part of the trip passed in that brain-dead haze that engulfs you after too many hours of travel. The bus continued to climb. Occasionally we passed through a darkened village or crossed over a bridge. Once as we drove through the forest I saw two moonlit silhouettes walking beside the road - those mysterious souls who always seem to be out before dawn in the middle of nowhere in Asian countries.

Then it was six o'clock and suddenly light - I must have drifted off as the sun came up. The bus was grinding its way up the hill from lower Dharamshala. Everyone was stretching, peering out of the window, putting their seats upright and getting their gear together. We drove past a military camp and wound further up through the forest. Then we were bumping our way over the potholed entrance to the bus station.

We had arrived in upper Dharamshala, also known as McLeod Ganj. Originally it was the home of the semi-nomadic Gaddi people, many of whom still live in the area. It became a hill station of the British Raj in 1848, but in 1905 a devastating earthquake killed 20,000 people in the region and destroyed most of the buildings in McLeod Ganj. After the disaster the area became a quiet backwater.

Forty-five years later, in 1950, Mao's Red Army invaded Tibet. The Dalai Lama escaped to India in 1959, followed over the next few months by thousands of Tibetans. The Indian government allowed His Holiness and the other refugees to settle in McLeod Ganj. In 1960 they established a government in exile there, now known as the Central Tibetan Administration. Fittingly, the word 'dharamshala' in Hindi means 'pilgrims' rest house' or 'sanctuary'.

It is strange to think that Dharamshala is only about a hundred kilometres from the Tibetan border, but a range of impenetrable mountains lies between the two.

The town of Dharamshala exists on two levels, separated by nine kilometres of road and about 550 metres in altitude. The lower town is the main market and has a large Indian population. Most of the Tibetans live in McLeod Ganj, known as 'McLo' for short.

The Englishwoman and I left the bus station together and walked up the hill to the town's tiny main square. There she pointed out the road I should take to reach Tibet Charity, past the Dalai Lama's temple. Feeling a little dazed and really hungry, I set off down Temple Road.

The first thing that struck me about McLeod Ganj was the state of the roadway. A mix of gravel, occasional patches of tar seal and a generous scattering of potholes made walking quite tricky, especially with a heavy pack.

There seemed to be a surprising number of people around for six-thirty in the morning. I know now that it's normal for people to be up and about early in India. Monks and nuns start their meditations well before daybreak. People selling bread and other food on the street set up their stalls before dawn, and many Tibetans go to the temple before they start the working day.

There was an air of quiet purpose - not a rush, but everyone seemed to know where they were going. On the whole, they appeared to be pretty cheerful about it. Several times I caught someone's eye and they gave me a warm smile. Most of the faces were Tibetan, weather beaten and red cheeked with the look of people who had spent most of their lives outdoors.

I wasn't quite sure if I was going the right way so I asked a woman, "Dalai Lama temple?" She smiled and pointed. "Dalai Lama temple." The narrow road hugged the edge of a steep cliff on one side and had a sheer drop off on the other. The cliff side of the street was lined with small shops and a couple of hotels, and a row of empty street stalls straggled down the other side.

I realised I had reached the temple, not because of any impressive façade - the gateway was flanked by an austere concrete arch - but because of the sudden concentration of activity in the area. It was obviously a focal point of the town.

Street sellers outside the gate were heating momos in steamers or laying out bundles of fresh vegetables. People were making their way through the gate into the temple complex. The wall beside the temple was plastered with colourful posters. A faded billboard carried a picture of a bewildered looking little boy and the words *Where is the Panchen Lama?*

A cow was rootling around in a large unsightly rubbish skip just metres from the temple entrance, and a bored policeman watched the action on the street. A couple of beggars wrapped in blankets approached me hopefully but I had no access to my money, so I gave them a "Sorry, another time" kind of grin and they backed off without protesting.

The simple map on the Tibet Charity website had indicated that I should go down the hill past the temple. The road suddenly became quite steep but also surprisingly busy, and I had quite a crowd of Tibetans around me as I started off down the hill. Some of them were turning prayer wheels.

I was puzzled when at the second corner they all left the

road, and set off purposefully along a narrow path into the forest. Luckily I spotted a man sitting on the balcony of an apartment building. I called out, "Tibet Charity?" and he pointed further down the road.

Within a couple of minutes I spotted a jumble of signs - *Starwud Kottage furnished rooms, Pause Dwelling* and *Snow Height Appartments Rooms Here.*

I knew that Snow Height Apartments was next door to Tibet Charity and I sincerely hoped I had a room waiting for me. My back ached from the weight of my pack, the long night's journey was definitely catching up with me, and I felt extremely thankful to have arrived.

## Chapter Three

# *Snow Height*

Snow Height's 'office' was a tiny shop packed with soft drinks, instant noodles, packets of biscuits, toilet paper and bottled water. The only occupant was a sleepy, squint-eyed Indian man who was obviously not expecting a new guest, or at least not that early. It was still only about 7 am.

It was a baffling encounter for both of us. We tried to communicate in English and got nowhere, then he tried Hindi - equally useless. At last he made a gesture to me to wait, had a hurried conversation on the phone, and within a few minutes had led me up to my room.

I dumped my pack thankfully on the polished stone floor, sat on the hard double bed and looked around my home for the next three months. The room was spacious enough for a couple of wooden lounge chairs, a TV on a low table and an old fashioned wooden wardrobe with a mirror. There was a small clean bathroom with a western style toilet, a shower and a hand basin. A tiny cubbyhole with a sink bench could be used as a kitchen. *Yes*, I thought. *I can live here. This feels fine.*

Outside my window was a little balcony and a superb view down the valley toward Lower Dharamshala and onward into a blue haze of distant hills. The scene was marred only by what looked like a small electrical sub-station directly opposite the apartment. Untidy power cables looped across the road to the various buildings.

Suddenly, there was a sharp whistling cry and a bird swooped past my window. I glimpsed a flash of blue and a pair of trailing black and white tail feathers longer than the bird's body, then it was gone.

I went out onto the balcony and leaned on the railing. The air was crisp and fresh. The strange bird had disappeared but high above I could see a dozen birds of prey riding the air currents. On my left, a pair of faded prayer flags fluttered over a building which I recognised from photos as Tibet Charity. In the distance was a stunning mountain range, bare rock towering into the sky and a tracery of tiny winding paths looping over the lower slopes.

I heard a tinkling of bells as down the hill came a parade of four donkeys. The leader stopped, apparently of his own accord, near a couple of heaps of gravel and bricks beside the road. They all stood gazing meditatively over the bank. Two men began loading gravel into the sacking panniers on the donkeys' backs. Once they were full, each donkey turned slowly, still deep in thought, ambled across the road and disappeared between the buildings. A few minutes later they reappeared, still at a leisurely pace, and headed back to the gravel pile. Every so often a car or motorbike would come careering down the hill. The donkeys paid not the slightest attention to the traffic, and the cars had to give way after tooting loudly to no avail.

A couple of passing Tibetan women waved up at me as they walked down the hill. An elderly Indian man nodded courteously from the balcony of the next door Pause Dwelling and called, "Good Morning!"

This was life on a Saturday morning in small town India and I found it fascinating. I was astonished to realise how relaxed I already felt in this place.

A European man came trudging heavily up the stairs from the little shop, carrying a bottle of fruit juice. On an impulse I said, "Excuse me, are you Andy?" All I knew about the other teachers at Tibet Charity was their names - Andy and Suzette from the USA, Lindy from Australia and Fleur from France.

The poor guy looked grey and drawn as he said yes, he was Andy. He added hastily that he had a stomach upset and needed to get back to his room on the floor above mine. As he indicated his balcony, an attractive auburn-haired woman in a bright Indian blouse appeared from the neighbouring doorway and cried, "Hey Gill. Welcome! I'm Suzette. So glad you're here!"

Andy scurried back to his room as Suzette and I made a date to walk up to town for breakfast.

"He's starting to get better," she said. "But he's been pretty miserable for the last couple of days. We all were sick at least once during the monsoon. You're so lucky to arrive today. This is the first fine day we've had in two months!"

*Chapter Four*

# *Saturday in Little Lhasa*

As we strolled up the road to breakfast, Suzette pointed out the mysterious forest track I had seen the Tibetans taking earlier in the morning.

"That's the kora, the pilgrim path around the Dalai Lama's temple. It's a beautiful walk."

I noticed Suzette walked very slowly and made frequent stops as we climbed the steep hill to town. She confessed to being a stereotypical American car addict, totally unused to walking. McLeod Ganj was at 1700 metres, so living at altitude and walking everywhere had been a real test for her. The monsoon had been particularly difficult, navigating potholed roads in the pouring rain.

"And it rains," she said, "For hours and hours on end. Your clothes won't dry, your shoes go mouldy, the electricity keeps going off. Some days it rained so much the students couldn't get to class."

I had made a mistake on my visa application and ended up with a three-month visa rather than the six-month one I thought I had applied for. This meant that I had avoided the monsoon. I felt rather lucky. The sun was shining, the sky was blue and cloudless - it looked as though it never rained at all.

We sat down in Café One-Two opposite the Dalai Lama's temple. Suzette immediately gave me a small bottle of hand sanitizer and advised me always to use it before meals. She had brought a huge bottle of the stuff from the USA and had taken it upon herself to make sure her fellow teachers were safe.

Cafés in McLeod Ganj have a simple but effective ordering system. The customer gets a menu, a piece of paper and a pencil, and writes down their own order and the price. It works brilliantly and saves a lot of confusion. I had fresh fruit, curd and muesli and delicious hot chocolate. I could see that finding good, cheap food in this town wasn't going to be a problem.

We finished our breakfast and continued our leisurely stroll toward the main part of town. By then the roadside stalls were all stocked and open. McLeod Ganj has been nicknamed 'Little Lhasa' and I could see why. Most of the stall holders were middle-aged Tibetan women in their traditional dress, the chuba, a full length wrap-around pinafore with a colourful blouse. The married women also wore a bright multi-striped apron.

The stallholders were sitting around chatting away, knitting or making jewellery using turquoise and polished gemstones. Some were threading tiny beads onto cotton to make colourful bracelets which read *Free Tibet.* They smiled and nodded as we paused to look at their merchandise, but there was no sense of a hard sell.

I told myself sternly to just look and not get carried away on my first day, but there was so much to see that I found it very hard to resist. The goods on the stalls seemed to be of pretty good quality. There was a selection of heavy antique necklaces and modern beaded jewellery. I spotted singing bowls of all sizes, statuettes of the Buddha and Ganesh the Hindu elephant god, heavy brass padlocks, wooden and brass boxes, colourful prayer flags and white khatas.

Several stalls were hung with soft yak wool rugs and scarves. Another sold Tibetan flags, colourful maps of Tibet, postcards of the Dalai Lama and scenes from around Dharamshala. A throaty chanting of "Om Mani Padme Hum" came from a stall selling CDs and DVDs. A young Indian with a tray offered us "Very good saffron, Madam". A couple of shoe-shine boys wanted to clean my sandals.

A cheerful club-footed beggar accosted me and I gave him a couple of coins. This was the start of an ongoing relationship with McLo's beggars. They were all Indians and most of them were either very old (at least they *looked* very old) or had a

14

deformity - blindness, no fingers, or deformed legs and feet. They were almost all friendly and polite, calling out "Hello Madam," as you passed and accepting with good grace if you didn't have any small notes or change to give them. There weren't many local beggars so it was possible to give something to all of them fairly regularly. The only time when begging became more of a problem was during the Dalai Lama's teachings. Then there were not only thousands of extra visitors in town but an influx of very insistent itinerant beggars, including children, and women with pathetic babies in their arms.

That first morning in McLo, Suzette and I had great fun browsing among the stalls and shops. A one-way street looped around the middle of town from the tiny main square, and you could cover the central shopping area at a leisurely pace in fifteen minutes. The only annoyance was the constant tooting of cars, tuk tuks and motorbikes as they negotiated their way down the narrow street, dodging people, dogs and cows.

On our way back to Snow Height came the best moment of the day. Around the square in front of the Dalai Lama's temple, the Tsuglag Khang, we found a crowd of Tibetans who lined the road down the hill as far as we could see.

"The Dalai Lama must be coming," said Suzette. "They always turn up when he drives in or out of the temple complex."

We joined the crowd beside the route, marked with a line of white paint on either side to keep away evil spirits. A few minutes later a convoy of SUVs swept up the hill. In the second car I caught sight of the Dalai Lama smiling broadly and nodding to the crowd. The Tibetans all stood with folded hands in an attitude of deep respect as he passed.

The Dalai Lama has described himself as a "professional laugher," and often talks about the power of a smile to break down barriers between strangers. He certainly has a very infectious smile, and I grinned all the way back to Snow Height. To see His Holiness on my first day seemed like a very positive omen.

# Chapter Five

# *Tibet Charity*

Over the next few days, I got to know my fellow teachers and the other people at Tibet Charity.

Suzette came from Los Angeles. She was in her early sixties but looked much younger. She had recently retired from her job as a school psychologist, and said she wanted more of a challenge out of life than editing her local community paper and cooking for her ninety-year-old "Mom".

Her application had initially been refused by Tibet Charity, but she had been called up with two weeks' notice when another teacher dropped out.

During her career in education, Suzette had worked in Alaska, Egypt and China. She told us about her brief marriage to a very young Chinese man whom she had met while teaching there. She had a droll, understated way of putting things and her account of meeting her Chinese in-laws had us in stitches. I thought she would make a great stand-up comedian.

Andy came from Salt Lake City, Utah. He was an outdoor type who loved hiking and physical exercise, and told me he had once spent six months in New Zealand, touring the country by bike. He was a career ESOL teacher who spent about half of each year teaching in Japan, so volunteer teaching in India was a busman's holiday for him.

Initially, I found Andy hard to like. He seemed rather brash, and often made loud offensive remarks when we were out together as a group, complaining about the barking dogs or the food or the state of the roads. He seemed to do this more for the effect that it had on other people, including embarrassing us, than because these things really upset him.

However, once I got to know Andy better and went on a couple of long walks with him, I began to enjoy his company. When I had a throat infection toward the end of term, it was Andy who showed the most concern and went to some trouble to fetch meals for me from town.

Lindy from Australia was glad I'd arrived because I could take over one of her two pre-intermediate classes. She was another career ESOL teacher who had worked in Kenya and various other countries. Her adventurous career had taken her into some difficult situations, and in fact it sounded as if she was lucky to be alive. She had been bitten by a pack of wild dogs in Romania and had not been given rabies injections. If the dogs had been rabid she almost certainly would have died.

I didn't have as much to do with Fleur, a young French-American, because she was one of those people who gets to know everyone and is involved in everything, so she had a very busy life in McLo.

Fleur taught English in Japan and was about to face a dilemma. She had applied for a university job for 2011 and had to go to Tokyo for an interview. She had a six-month visa for India, but if she left the country she would not be allowed to return for two months. She loved Dharamshala and desperately wanted to stay, but she also needed the job in Japan. Eventually, after much soul searching, she decided she had to go. She left about a fortnight after I arrived.

There were also three Tibetan teachers at Tibet Charity. Pema and Norbu did the important job of teaching the absolute beginners, people who had come out of Tibet with no English at all and had to start from ABC. Once they were ready for elementary level English they went into the classes taken by the foreign volunteer teachers.

Pema was a serious young woman who had done her teacher training in India. As well as teaching, she also took care of the day-to-day running of the English School. Norbu had spent many years in America where he had been a carpenter, before training as a teacher and returning to India.

17

The third Tibetan teacher was Sonam, a cheery young guy who did a heroic job of teaching basic computer skills in a cramped classroom full of elderly machines. He also managed the charity's website.

Our other contacts at Tibet Charity were The Director, Dekyi and Mr Moon.

Everyone always addressed the Director by his title. He was happy to see the foreign teachers but had little to do with the school except on special occasions. He had a lot on his mind, as Tibet Charity not only had projects in various parts of India but also in Nepal and Ladakh, working in the areas of education, old people's welfare and animal health.

The Director was a dog lover, and took a special interest in the vet programme for de-sexing dogs and vaccinating them against rabies. The Brigitte Bardot Foundation is one of Tibet Charity's major sponsors and donates thousands of euros each year for the animal health programme.

The vet clinic was on the other side of town, but all other aspects of Tibet Charity were housed in the building next to Snow Height. These included the administration, the English school and the nursing school. A dozen home nursing students were being trained to care for old people in their homes, using naturopathy and Ayurvedic medicine. We used to meet the lively young nursing students at lunch every day.

Dekyi the cook was an older woman who spoke very little English but had a beautiful smile. Every day she would serve up the same vegetarian lunch - rice, dahl and a green vegetable. One of the first things I learned in Tibetan was "Shim-po duk" (it's delicious), which was worth saying just to watch Dekyi's shy grin. The free lunch was Tibet Charity's gesture of thanks to the volunteers; otherwise we covered all our own expenses.

The other English teachers told me it would take about six weeks before I couldn't stand eating the same food every day, and this turned out to be absolutely right. As my enthusiasm for dahl and rice waned, I used to watch the nursing students

18

tucking into their lunch with gusto, spicing up their food with liberal spoonfuls of chilli paste and thoroughly enjoying every mouthful.

As for me, I started having lunch in town most days, although I continued to eat at the school at least once a week because I didn't want to hurt Dekyi's feelings. The food was perfectly good - it was just that I had grown up in the opulent West and was used to a more varied diet.

Tibet Charity's caretaker was Dawa, which translates as 'moon', so the foreign teachers called him Mr Moon. He had a passion for motorcycles and could often be seen roaring around town on his powerful bike. I accepted a lift on the pillion once and was terrified as we roared down the hill. From then on, I politely refused any more offers of a ride.

Once a month, the Director, the staff and the volunteers would have an evening meal together at Tibet Charity. Mr Moon did the cooking for these gatherings, and the menu always included a delicious mutton stew.

The Director, his family and Mr Moon all lived on the upper floors of the building, along with the Director's ancient cataract-ridden pet dog. There were also three ex-strays who had found themselves in doggy heaven. They lived on the terrace in front of the main entrance and were regularly fed huge bowls of food by Mr Moon.

One of the dogs, Tenzin, had bitten a student just before I arrived and the Director had rather reluctantly agreed to tie him up. The other dogs used to roam freely around the building and they occasionally came into the classrooms.

It's not easy to maintain your dignity as a teacher when a dog is determined to stick its nose into your lap.

*Chapter Six*

# *I start school*

I had a very gentle introduction to teaching. On Monday, I met my pre-intermediate students and watched as Lindy took the class. World Rabies Day celebrations would take place on Tuesday, so my real teaching duties would not start until Wednesday.

I also took my first conversation class with Suzette. These classes were voluntary and available to students of any level, so they included people with quite advanced English skills as well as those who hardly spoke any English at all.

Attendance at conversation classes varied, but we had about twenty students that day. We divided the students into two groups and Suzette kindly gave me the more advanced group for my first lesson.

We sat in a circle and eyed one another expectantly - the fifty-seven-year-old Kiwi and the young Tibetans, some in maroon monks' robes, most in casual jeans and trainers.

I began by giving the students a quick rundown of my life. Born in New Zealand, married with two sons, spent three years in Denmark, so I had some experience of living in a foreign country and learning a new language. Had been briefly in Delhi many years ago but had not travelled around India until now, and was excited about coming to Dharamshala. Someone asked where Denmark and New Zealand were, and we found them on the wall map. New Zealand, we all agreed, was a long way away.

Then I said, "Now, please could you tell me about yourselves. How did you get to Dharamshala?"

Cheerful young Mingma already knew me from the pre-intermediate class, so he began. He had been born in India and educated in a monastery, he said. After his father died his mother had become a Buddhist nun. Mingma and his sister cared for their elderly grandfather, and had come to Dharamshala so the old man could be near the Dalai Lama and study the Dharma.

Tenzin had also been born in India, and was a travel agent who usually worked in Varanasi. He already spoke several languages but wanted to improve his English. Ironically it was Tenzin who had been bitten a few days earlier by his namesake, one of Tibet Charity's resident strays.

Another student whom I recognised from the pre-intermediate class was a monk, Lobsang. He told us how he had fled Tibet with his cousin thirteen years before, when he was eighteen. It took them three weeks to walk over the mountains to Nepal, constantly afraid of being caught by Chinese border patrols.

"Is the rest of your family still in Tibet?" I asked. Quietly Lobsang replied that he had only been able to speak to his nomad parents twice by phone in all the time he had been in India. His cousin had since gone back to Tibet and had been arrested - just for being a monk.

Nawang, another monk, told us he had been caught by Nepali border guards and handed over to the Chinese. His first two months in prison were very hard, he said, and he was often beaten. As he spoke my attention was drawn to a long scar on his shaven head. Later he was allowed to work in the garden and prison life became "not too bad."

Eventually Nawang's father paid quite a large sum of money to secure his release. He made it to India on his second attempt.

Nima was an anxious looking woman in her thirties. Her lack of confidence in speaking English made her story difficult to understand, but with the help of the others I learned that she had come over the mountains with a small group of people in winter. Travelling in winter is quite common because it's easier to avoid the border patrols, but it makes the journey on foot much more dangerous.

One day they met up with some Maoist Shining Path guerrillas who gave them food, and they made it safely to Kathmandu where all the escapees are processed before being bussed to India.

Sitting together were two sweet young girls, Jigmey and Dechen. I tried to guess their ages and thought they couldn't be more than eighteen.

Dechen had such an infectious grin that I couldn't help smiling as she told us about her journey. She had travelled in a group of eighty people, ranging in age from three months to sixty years. Because there are various dialects in Tibet and nobody else came from Dechen's village, she couldn't even talk to her fellow travellers at first.

The group took several months to get from Lhasa to Dharamshala. They had to move carefully because travelling in such large numbers increased the risk of being caught. They crossed the mountains in winter, had to hide from the border patrols many times, and had run out of food by the time they reached Nepal.

Dechen's friend Jigmey's story had an ironic twist. Once she and her companions reached Kathmandu they were all given a health check before going on to India. The examination revealed that Jigmey, who had just climbed over some really daunting mountain passes, had a serious heart condition. She ended up in a Delhi hospital having open heart surgery which probably saved her life.

I looked around the circle of young students and thought about what I had heard. I tried to imagine leaving my own family, climbing high mountain passes in winter, facing fear, hunger and frostbite, not to mention possible arrest and imprisonment, all in search of an uncertain future.

All I could think of to say was, "You're so brave," and they actually looked a little embarrassed.

"So," I added, after a little pause, "Do you want to go back to Tibet one day?"

Of course they did, they said, surprised at the question. Whatever hardships they experience in exile, they know they are the lucky ones. "And one day Tibet will be free," they said with certainty.

One positive effect of this conversation was that I stopped agonising about why I had come to Dharamshala. After hearing the students' stories, I realised that the answer was obvious.

They wanted to learn English. So all *I* had to do was a good job in the classroom. It was as simple as that.

*Chapter Seven*

# The dogs get jabbed and I get educated

The teachers and students were expected to turn up at Tibet Charity the following morning to celebrate World Rabies Day; then we had the rest of the day off. We all gathered in the dining room and waited an hour for something to happen. Eventually a couple of cars drew up outside and the Director ushered in the special guests. They included the Chief Vet of the state of Himachal Pradesh, and a representative from the Central Tibetan Administration.

The World Rabies Day ceremony gave me a crash course into this frightening infection and its deadly consequences.

The Director spoke first and related how the Dalai Lama had initiated the rabies programme some years ago. His Holiness had insisted that something needed to be done about the many stray dogs in Dharamshala, both for the sake of the animals' own health and because they are major transmitters of rabies to humans.

Buddhists believe that it is wrong to take a life. In the West the answer would probably have been to kill the dogs as humanely as possible, but here in India another solution had to be found.

Tibet Charity developed a programme for de-sexing the strays, treating them for injuries and diseases and vaccinating them annually against rabies. Over time, the number of stray dogs is expected to decrease naturally, and there are already fewer strays in the area. The Charity's Tibetan vets are joined from time to time by volunteers from other countries, who take the programme to villages around the state.

The Chief Vet spoke about the rabies problem in India, and I was startled to learn that fifteen million people each year are bitten by animals capable of transmitting rabies. These include monkeys, bats, dogs, mongooses and cows, although over ninety percent of the bites are from dogs. Thirty thousand people a year die of rabies in India alone.

The nursing tutor then gave a PowerPoint presentation with English language visuals which she translated into Tibetan for the students, stressing the need to clean the wound and go to a doctor as soon as possible after being bitten. I glanced at Lindy who was looking tense, remembering her experience in Romania with the wild dogs.

After the speeches, we all trooped outside to the terrace where Tenzin and the two other strays-in-residence received their annual rabies jab from the Chief Vet, to a round of applause. Tibet Charity was celebrating Rabies Day by offering free injections to pet dogs, and a crowd of Tibetans had arrived with their dogs on leads, mostly a small white hairy breed called the Lhasa apso.

The formal part of the day seemed to be over, so after a cup of tea and a biscuit we left the vets to it.

As I was walking through town that afternoon, I was handed a leaflet about a talk at *Learning and Ideas for Tibet*, one of several volunteer organisations in McLo. That evening I went along to hear a first-hand account of the 2008 uprising in Tibet. I vaguely remembered hearing about this on the news in New Zealand, but had no idea of what had really happened.

The small meeting room was crowded with Europeans of all ages. The guest speaker, Jampa, had his arm in a sling. He spoke in Tibetan and his words were translated by one of his countrymen. This man bore a remarkable resemblance to the film star Ewan McGregor. However, I quickly dismissed such a frivolous thought as Jampa began his story.

He started by giving us a general picture of life in Tibet under the Chinese. From 1950 when they invaded, and particularly after the Dalai Lama's flight in 1959, things became increasingly difficult for the Tibetan people. The Chinese government made the farmers grow wheat instead of barley, resulting in huge crop failures and widespread famine. They interfered with the nomad yak herders' traditional way of life. Millions of Han Chinese were encouraged to emigrate to Tibet, where they were given the best jobs.

As a result, Tibetans are now outnumbered in their own country and live as second-class citizens. Even the future of the Tibetan language is under threat, because the children are taught mainly in Mandarin.

From the Tibetan point of view, the worst blow of all has probably been the desecration of their religion. Shortly after the invasion, Mao told the Dalai Lama, "Religion is poison." The young Dalai Lama admired many aspects of Marxist philosophy, but he began to realise that Tibetan Buddhism and those who practised it were in great danger.

In the years after the Dalai Lama escaped from Tibet, six thousand monasteries were destroyed, their treasures stolen or battered to pieces, and many monks and nuns were publicly humiliated, imprisoned or killed.

Even now, Tibetans can be arrested for saying the Dalai Lama's name or having a picture of him. The six-year-old Panchen Lama, whose photo appears so poignantly outside the Dalai Lama's temple in McLo, was kidnapped by the Chinese government and has not been seen for twenty years.

Despite all this hardship, the Tibetan people have been remarkably staunch about preserving their religion, their traditions and their Buddhist philosophy of nonviolence. For years they had no news of the Dalai Lama and many feared he could be dead. Despite their isolation and Chinese attempts to suppress their religion, they continued to practise Buddhism, go on pilgrimages and support the few monks left in the desecrated monasteries.

It's only in the past few years that the internet and mobile phones have revolutionised communication, so Tibetans inside the country now have more contact with their family members in exile. They are also more aware of the widespread sympathy for their plight from people in many countries around the world.

Tibetans are generally a long-suffering, optimistic and peace-loving people, but once in a while they rise up against their oppressors in fervent but mostly nonviolent protest. This usually happens around 10 March.

On that day in 1959, now known as Tibet Uprising Day, a huge crowd of Tibetans surrounded the Norbulingka Palace in Lhasa to protect the Dalai Lama, who they feared was about to be abducted by the Chinese. A tense standoff arose. Many of the Tibetans were armed. The Chinese brought in heavy artillery and a few days later they began shelling the palace.

The Dalai Lama and his family made a daring night-time escape from Lhasa and arrived in India after a dangerous journey over the mountains. In the months and years that followed, thousands of people within Tibet were killed or arrested and many Tibetans joined their leader in exile.

March 10 has been the rallying point for a number of demonstrations since 1959. On that date in 2008, monks from Sera and Drepung monasteries assembled in front of the Jokhang temple in Lhasa, calling for human rights, religious freedom and the return of the Dalai Lama.

Within a few days, the protests had spread to other parts of Tibet. They were mostly peaceful, although there were a few incidents in which Chinese people were attacked. In some places, protesters smashed windows in government offices and Chinese businesses.

Monks, nuns and ordinary Tibetans in villages all round the country defied the authorities as they gathered in spontaneous demonstrations, expressing their support for the Dalai Lama and calling for a free Tibet.

"Now you know how things are in my country, I will tell you *my* story," said Jampa.

He told us he came from Kham province in eastern Tibet, and had first-hand experience of Chinese oppression within his own family. His elderly grandfather had been imprisoned for seven months for possessing a portrait of the Dalai Lama.

In March 2008, Jampa joined a protest outside a nunnery in his village and said he saw a monk fall to the ground, shot by the police. He ran to help and was himself shot twice, through the body and the arm. In the confusion, his friends managed to get him onto a motorbike and fled with him up into the hills above the village.

Jampa lay up in the mountains for over a year with very little treatment for his wounds beyond what his friends could fetch for him. He described in graphic detail how his arm had become rotten and maggoty, and they had had to cut away the infected areas. He gingerly unwrapped his arm. It was clearly useless and still gave him a lot of pain.

After the protests, the Chinese accused Jampa of being an agitator and put him on their *Most Wanted* list. Once he was well enough to move around, his friends arranged for him to escape to India, along with his close friend Tsering who had risked his own life to help him. Both of them had to leave their families behind. Jampa left his mother, his wife and his two children in Tibet. He finally made it to Dharamshala in May 2009.

I glanced around the room and could see I was not the only one to be profoundly moved by Jampa's story. He told us he had had very little education, but he spoke well. He was impassioned and very sincere. He cared deeply about Tibet and desperately wanted to share his story with as many people as possible.

Afterwards, I walked thoughtfully back to Snow Height through the darkened town.

# Chapter Eight

# *Ra-tas, La-tas and Ya-tas*

I made a useful contact the night of Jampa's talk. While eating dinner in the Peace Café I shared a table with Paul, a lanky, long-haired young Texan who was studying Buddhist philosophy and learning Tibetan at the Tibet Library. He lived at Pause Dwelling next door to Snow Height, so the following morning we met up and walked down the steep road to the Library. I wanted to find out about joining the Tibetan language class.

The Library of Tibetan Works and Archives was the most eye-catching building in the haphazard jumble which made up the Central Tibetan Administration complex. It had a stunning façade painted with brightly coloured murals. At one end appeared a vivid depiction of the Wheel of Life, and at the other was a representation of the Path to Enlightenment. Life-sized paintings of two seated figures flanked the door - one a famous king of Tibet and the other a respected translator of Buddhist texts.

The Library houses many precious manuscripts and also has a small museum, so for the Tibetans it's a sacred treasure house. A number of elderly men and women were walking around the building in a clockwise direction, turning prayer wheels or fingering their loops of prayer beads and muttering mantras. Several stray dogs were sprawled comfortably on the Library steps, fast asleep in the sun.

I inquired at the reception desk about joining the Tibetan class. The receptionist said I could have a free lesson to see if I liked it before signing up for the term.

The class was taught by Ani-la, a middle-aged Tibetan nun. She wasted no time on anything as frivolous as greetings, and we launched straight into chanting the thirty Tibetan consonants, "Ka kha ga nga" and so on down to "Ha ah!"

It seemed there were four vowel sounds and any number of Ra-tas, La-tas, Ran-gos, Ya-tas, Wa-surs, heavy letters, Sanskrit letters, prefixes, suffixes and post-suffixes to be learned by heart. I shared a textbook with Areva, a beautiful but fragile young Thai woman, and thought it all looked incredibly complicated. The class had already been going for two weeks but they had only covered about five pages, so I decided I would probably be able to catch up.

There was a welcome moment of comic relief when Ani-la drew a zebra on the board to demonstrate the "Za" sound. She taught in very broken English and her class included Russians, a Swede, Koreans, Germans, Thais and Indians, all with various levels of proficiency in English, so she sometimes had quite an uphill battle to get her point across.

After the class, I signed up for three month's worth of lessons and laboured up the hill again. It took half an hour with various panting stops 'to admire the view' and I could see I needed to get a lot fitter.

Just down the road from Snow Height was a very decrepit café called Open Sky - well named, since the roof was full of holes. I ordered a chai and got out my notebook to practise the Tibetan letters. An old monk sitting at the next table gave me a charming, toothless grin and kindly helped me to write and pronounce the first few consonants.

Unfortunately, Open Sky's chai turned out to be as dodgy as its roof. After a queasy afternoon I decided to avoid the café in future, so I missed out on any further tutoring from the friendly old monk.

Tibetan class actually turned out to be quite fun. We crawled through the various letters and sounds for several lessons and then suddenly accelerated into sentences. The first one we learned was "This is a Yak" (Di yak re).

With Ani-la we learned the basic written language and discovered its eccentricities. One of these is that although each *syllable* in a sentence is separated by a dot, nobody seems to

30

have considered that it might be a good idea to put gaps between the *words*.

Unfortunately, our textbook didn't include many useful everyday phrases and the course wasn't geared toward spoken Tibetan. Even "Di yak re" wasn't any good, as yaks are high altitude animals and there were none in Dharamshala. By the end of three months, I could translate written sentences like *The dog is under the car* and *I met you yesterday in the market*. However, I could only ask, "How much is it?" because I'd learned it from a phrase book, and I usually couldn't understand the answer.

I found out rather late in the term that there actually was a class in spoken Tibetan. However, it only accepted people who had a basic grasp of the written language, which was what we were studying with Ani-la.

Our class was quite a mixed bunch. There was a Korean monk who always sat in the front row. He really excelled at chanting the thirty consonants, La-tas, Ran-gos and so on, which we did at the start of every lesson. He went back to Korea toward the end of term, and we suddenly found ourselves embarrassed by the realisation of how much he'd been carrying us along. Ani-la was clearly disgusted at the sudden drop in chanting quality.

Another Korean monk used to invariably wander in late, and sit with a beatific smile on his face all through the lesson. I never saw him take any notes, and for a while I thought he might be an inspector sent to monitor the class. However, he was part of the group who sat the exam at the end of the year, which was the first time I saw him lift a pen.

There were a number of earnest young European women learning Tibetan, including a Swede with whom I sometimes used to walk up the hill after class. She had been in Dharamshala for several months studying Buddhist philosophy, and had a part-time job as a nanny for a Danish couple. Most of the time I knew her she had a nagging respiratory infection and I used to get quite concerned about her health. As the weather got cooler she seemed to get better, so just when most people were starting to hoik and cough in the wintry air she looked quite rosy and fit.

One of the more colourful members of the class was a middle-aged German with a sunny smile and a weather-beaten complexion. She was liberally hung about with jangling bracelets and prayer beads, and always wore the same bright blue brocade chuba - the sort of costume Tibetan women would only wear on special occasions. Since she usually arrived late to class and hurried away afterwards, I never got to know anything about her. I used to wonder about her background and what had brought her to Dharamshala.

Irma from Tuva was another enigma. She was a woman in her sixties with striking Mongolian features. I thought I was having trouble learning Tibetan, but I realised my problems were minimal compared to Irma's. Our textbook was in English but she spoke no more than half a dozen words. Armed with a huge English/Russian dictionary, she would laboriously translate the next few pages of the textbook into Russian every night. It was the only way she could have any idea of what was going on in class. She told me, mostly in sign language, that she was learning Tibetan so she could study the precious texts in the Tibet Library.

As a fellow teacher, I really admired Ani-la's patience and dedication. She had a difficult job teaching basic Tibetan to such a wide range of people. Once I got used to her brisk demeanour and learned to interpret her broken English, I enjoyed her classes.

Ani-la had quite a sense of humour and would often use drawings to demonstrate a point. One day she drew a yak and three identical objects that looked like bowler hats. She used these to illustrate her assertion that yak butter was far superior to cow or sheep butter.

During another lesson when we were tackling *It is as cold as hell today!* she drew a penguin and told us about the poor freezing Emperor penguin, carrying his egg on his feet in the Antarctic blizzards. *March of the Penguins* has obviously had a very wide audience. Whenever we talked about animals in

32

my conversation class, someone was always bound to mention penguins.

Another little story originated from the question, "Do you like sweet tea?" Ani-la built up a scenario in which a Tibetan entertains their overseas sponsor who has travelled all the way to India to meet the object of their generosity.

I don't know how much money overseas sponsors pump into the economy of the Tibetans in exile, but it must be quite substantial. When I checked the internet I found opportunities to sponsor children, nuns and monks, elderly people, hermits, performing arts students and disabled people. Sponsorship by foreign supporters is one of the ways in which the Tibetan community in exile has been able to keep itself going over the years.

Getting to and from Tibetan class was always interesting. I would usually walk down the road in the morning and take the track up through the forest after class.

The road wound down the mountainside toward lower Dharamshala. On a clear day from a vantage point above the Library you got a good view of the town's cricket stadium. It was a massive modern construction which dominated the townscape and reflected the enormous popularity of the game in India.

The lower town itself was a chaotic mass of shops, people, scattered rubbish and traffic jams which did not attract me at all, so I never went there except to drive through it.

Almost everyone I met as I walked down the road would exchange a smile and a greeting - "Tashi delek" with the Tibetans and "Namaste" with the Indians.

Quite often I would come across troops of monkeys, the babies chittering excitedly and swinging madly through the trees beside the roadway. One morning, I was coming up the steep path from the Library when I met a Tibetan chatting away on his mobile as he walked. Just behind him a large monkey was knuckling its way purposefully down the path. They just happened to be going in the same direction.

Monks and nuns were common on the road. There was an old Tibetan woman who used to wear the most beautiful hand-embroidered felt boots. Groups of Indian construction workers, mostly women with gold nose rings and brightly coloured cotton saris, would be making their way up the hill to their latest job as I came down in the morning.

Every day I would walk through Jogiwara village, a tiny cluster of houses with a busy motorcycle workshop, a barber's and a miniscule café. One morning I noticed that the doorway of one of the houses was decorated with bright orange garlands of marigolds. A wedding was underway, and the guests were arriving in their best clothes. Inside the house a band was playing loudly and energetically at a terrific pace, like an Indian version of Spike Jones.

Occasionally the air would be full of clouds of smoke and the choking smell of hot asphalt, as a gang of road menders cooked up the sticky mixture over a fire by the roadside. I often met the donkey construction gang at various places along the road, going off to their latest job or standing stoically while the men loaded their panniers with gravel or bricks. There was a huge amount of building going on and the donkey gang was in hot demand.

As September turned into October, I noticed bright patches of pink on the hillsides. I was surprised to find that they were trees laden with blossom. It seemed odd to see blossom in the lead-up to the cold season, but I suppose nature takes advantage of a window of opportunity before the really cold weather sets in.

Then, in November, as the weather got drier and cooler, the walk through the forest was punctuated by the sound of chopping as people hacked thin branches off the trees for animal feed. Men and women trudged down the tracks, bowed down by enormous loads of branches so the only visible part of them was their feet.

There was always something new to see and puzzle over. A typical entry in my diary reads:

*After class I walked up through the forest and met a lizard, some beautiful butterflies, five cows, four monkeys and a gaggle of Tibetan nuns, all smiles as they chattered their way down the hill.*

# Chapter Nine

# *Life in the classroom*

It didn't take long to settle into a teaching routine with my students at Tibet Charity. The numbers varied at first as people came and left, but in the end I found myself with eight regulars in the afternoon pre-intermediate class.

We met in a small classroom on the second floor. The facilities were basic but adequate. The students' chairs were the type with an individual desk-cum-armrest attached. There was a CD player which we used for listening practice, a whiteboard and a good supply of whiteboard markers. The school's budget evidently didn't stretch to proper erasers, as there was a rather grubby and insanitary cloth for wiping the board.

The main drawback about teaching in McLo was that you never knew when the electricity would go off. When this happened we would all edge closer to the windows to catch the light, and I would have to improvise listening exercises in the absence of the CD player.

The Tibet Charity course used the Oxford University Press *New English File* textbooks, and we were expected to work our way through the book in a four-and-a-half month term. Since we only taught two hours a day we had to move quite steadily through the textbook, and there was really no time for any extra activities to vary the lessons. I found it a bit restrictive, but the students seemed to appreciate the structured approach of a textbook.

As I got to know my students better, I gradually came to understand how limited their early education had been. Those who had grown up in nomadic communities had only had about three years of schooling in Tibet, so their efforts to learn English were really impressive.

Their mobile phones were much fancier than mine, but their knowledge of the world beyond the Tibetan community was generally quite unsophisticated. Most of them seemed to know little about the American and Euro-centric world we encountered in our textbook.

One day we read a story about a couple ejecting their 20-something children from home because they had outlived their welcome. The students clearly found this quite puzzling. The idea was alien to them, partly because in Dharamshala there is no spare accommodation and no money to pay for such luxuries as separate flats, even if families don't all want to live together.

I also got the sense that although young Tibetans may disagree with their elders - for example many young Tibetans are irritated by the Dalai Lama's Middle Way policy of nonviolence in dealing with China - they still retain a genuine respect for older people.

I enjoyed my lessons with the pre-intermediates. They all had a very positive attitude toward learning English and were fun to be with, so I used to look forward to our classes each afternoon.

Nineteen-year-old Mingma, bright, funny and articulate, was the undoubted star of the show. He hardly ever skipped lessons, always did his homework and had a perpetual grin. Whenever I had real trouble explaining a grammatical point in English, Mingma would willingly take over in Tibetan.

Pemba was a good friend of Mingma's. He told me he had left his home in Tibet without telling his family he was planning to escape to India, and crossed the mountains with only a paid guide for company.

Tragically Pemba's mother had died the previous year. Because he had come out of Tibet illegally, he couldn't get a pass to return. He often seemed sad and preoccupied, but would have endearing flashes of humour and fun.

One of the first to arrive each afternoon was Dawa, a young woman in her twenties with a shy giggle and an annoying mobile phone which she often forgot to turn off. Dawa had clearly not had a lot of education and was a very slow reader and writer. She had a lovely nature and was certainly willing enough, but both of us sometimes found it a bit of a struggle.

Dorje was a quiet young monk with a limp. He worked hard whenever he came to class, but his attendance was too sporadic for him to do really well. A couple of times he asked me to read some quite poetic English writing in a small notebook, and I was puzzled by the difference in quality from his class work. The book turned out to belong to a friend.

Dolkar also took quite a bit of time off, but she had a good excuse as she and her husband had a busy street stall where they sold clothes, kitchenware, incense and packaged food. Every so often Dolkar would have to mind the stall for a few days while her husband went to Delhi to buy new stock. Her spoken English was quite good because she got plenty of practice talking to tourists, and she worked hard in class. Like Mingma, she was a jolly sort and always good for a laugh.

Lobsang was one of my more frustrating students because the quality of his work varied so much. He was a monk who had been in a monastery in South India for several years before coming to Dharamshala. When he set himself to it he worked very well and often asked intelligent questions in class, but I had trouble persuading him to do his homework or study seriously for tests.

Lobsang often wore a woollen hat. My first (and, to be honest, virtually my only) breakthrough in understanding spoken Tibetan happened one day when he came back to class after the tea break and exclaimed, "I've left my hat outside!" - or something like that - in Tibetan.

"Shamo!" I exclaimed. "Hat. I understood!" The class was delighted.

Suchin, my only non-Tibetan student, had come from Bangkok to study at Tibet Charity. There were a number of Thai Buddhist monks and lay students in town, who studied Buddhist philosophy as well as English. As foreigners they paid more to attend the classes, but apparently it was still cheaper than studying in Thailand.

Suchin worked hard, although she was often a few minutes late to class and would rush in breathlessly, to the laughter of the other students.

Tibetans love teasing each other and they really enjoy a joke at someone else's expense. The class would laugh at Dawa when she made mistakes, and she always took this very good naturedly. However, as the term went on, they would often say, "Dawa's getting better, isn't she, teacher?" and I really warmed to them.

They thoroughly enjoyed my occasional tussles with the CD player, and I used to exaggerate my sighs of frustration or little yelps when I played the wrong track, because they found them so funny.

I thought the Tibetans were generally an attractive people with their high cheekbones and brown faces, but Lhamo of the long dark hair and gorgeous smile was particularly beautiful. She was twenty-one and had married a young Dutchman the year before. Unfortunately, her husband had gone back to Holland and Lhamo was stuck in Dharamshala waiting for a visa to join him. I would often see her in the evening, leaning over the balcony at Pause Dwelling talking to him on her mobile. Lhamo was the first to invite me to her apartment, where she cooked a delicious lunch of mutton momos and showed me photos of her blonde, long-haired husband.

Lhamo was not alone in her quest to move on and find a secure future. It's not easy being a Tibetan in exile.

The Dalai Lama frequently talks about the generosity of the Indian government in accepting him and his fellow Tibetans as refugees in 1959, and continuing to receive the ongoing flow of escapees from Tibet over the years. It was an astonishing gesture, actually, considering the political ramifications, and it certainly hasn't improved India's long-term relationship with China.

Tibetan refugees in India are issued with Residential Certificates which have to be renewed every year. Those born in India are able to apply for citizenship, but many choose not to do this because it means renouncing their Tibetan nationality.

If they want to travel overseas temporarily, the Tibetans are issued with a special identity document from the Indian government, but this is not a passport and it's not always recognised by Customs officers in other countries.

The Director told us about a trip he and his wife had made to Denmark in 2009. At Munich airport they were detained and subjected to hours of humiliating questions by officials who didn't believe their travel permits were valid. The incident had left its mark and he was clearly still angry and frustrated about what had happened.

Tibetans also face problems if they want to establish themselves in business. In some Indian states, including Himachal Pradesh, Tibetans and other foreigners are not allowed to buy or own land. This makes it difficult for them to plan for their long-term future.

It's understandable that many of the people who escape to India from Tibet eventually move to other countries to seek better educational and economic opportunities. Of the 128,000 Tibetans currently in exile[1] about 34,000 are based outside India.

---

[1] Information from the *Demographic Survey of Tibetans in Exile 2009* (Planning Commission, Central Tibetan Administration.)

Of the 34,000 Tibetans in exile outside India, only 66 are living in New Zealand (2006 Census). This includes around twenty children.

According to Friends of Tibet New Zealand, the Tibetans who have come to New Zealand gained entry on work visas or through marriage with NZ citizens. Up to now New Zealand has not accepted Tibetans as part of its refugee quota, despite lobbying from Friends of Tibet New Zealand.

The New Zealand government is rather smug about being one of only twenty countries to operate an annual refugee quota, but in fact it only totals 750 people a year (0.017% of our population).

It's interesting to consider that if New Zealand's percentage of Tibetan refugees was the same as India's, we would have welcomed 2500 Tibetans to this country.

# Chapter Ten

# *Of monks and monkeys*

One of the things that worried me a little before I went to India (though not as much as whether I would get terrible diarrhoea, step on a snake or be bitten by a rabid dog) was how I would relate to any monks I had to teach.

I had only ever encountered Tibetan monks at various arts festivals in New Zealand when they were painstakingly making sand mandalas, a sacred activity requiring a lot of concentration. They seemed to be gentle people, intense and self-contained, and I'd been slightly reassured to hear that two young monks at Taupo Arts festival had tried water skiing. This seemed to indicate they had a lighter side, but I hadn't personally encountered it.

I was a little concerned about how I should deal with monks in the classroom. Having read Kipling's *Kim,* I had the idea that they preferred to keep their distance from women. If I was checking their work, would they be offended if I touched them? Were there subjects I shouldn't talk about? Would they be very pious and serious? What if they tried to convert me to Buddhism?

As it happened, one of the first questions I was asked (by a monk) in my initial conversation class was, "Are you a Buddhist?" However, when I said I wasn't, we just moved on to talk about other things. I think it was probably a standard question because so many of the visitors to Dharamshala *are* Buddhists.

As I read more about Buddhism, I realised that it's not a proselytizing religion like Islam or Christianity, and nobody made any attempt to convert me. In fact, I occasionally wished they would, as it might have made it easier to satisfy my growing curiosity about Buddhist philosophy and practice.

The monks with whom I had the most contact were Dorje and Lobsang in my pre-intermediate group, and the ones in the conversation class. I was relieved to find that, apart from their maroon robes and shaven heads, they were not actually very different from any of my other students. They enjoyed a laugh, were relaxed with me and got on well with the other students.

I have always been rather tickled by the similarity of the words *monk* and *monkey*. One of my favorite photos from Dharamshala shows a monk (Tibetan - *trapa*) walking down the road toward the kora, watched by a monkey (Tibetan - *piu*) in a tree.

One day in conversation class we were talking about a nearby monastery. It was surrounded by trees, and someone said you had to be careful of the monkeys who lived outside the monastery grounds.

"So there are monks inside the monastery and monkeys outside it?" I asked. There was a pause while the students made the linguistic connection and then they roared with laughter.

Occasionally we showed DVDs to the whole school, about half of whom were monks. Reading the English subtitles gave the students some useful comprehension practice. One day we showed the film *Mongol*. Toward the end of the film there was a cosy domestic scene between Temujin (the young Ghengis Khan) and his wife.

Suddenly the film jumped forward to a totally unrelated scene. I looked over at Norbu who was operating the DVD projector. He just shrugged and the movie continued uninterrupted until the power went off and we had to abandon the screening. Norbu later told me he'd skipped over a sex scene so as not to offend the monks. I was amused by the fact that the monks had actually seemed captivated and not at all bothered by some pretty gruesome scenes of fighting and slaughter.

Another evening there was a fashion show at TIPA. I was not feeling well and didn't go. I was sorry to miss it as my student Lhamo was one of the models, but Lindy reported back on what had happened. The show had included original costumes based on traditional designs as well as some quite skimpy modern clothing.

"The monks," she said, "Were really loving it, shouting out comments, whistling and carrying on. It was amazing!"

Most of the Tibet Charity monks had come from monasteries in South India. They were sent to Dharamshala especially to learn English. Life in the monasteries is very disciplined. However, while they were in Dharamshala they stayed in apartments, cooked their own meals and lived a much less regulated life.

On Mondays when we had a "What did you do at the weekend?" discussion, I found the monk students' weekend schedule pretty much resembled my own - washing clothes, doing some shopping, going for a walk and watching TV…

The majority of the monks who lived in Dharamshala were based at the various local monasteries. I had heard they worked very hard, waking early in the morning and spending long hours in study and meditation. The monastery just up the hill from Snow Height used to ring a waking bell at around 3.30am, and you could hear the faint sound of monks chanting as the sun came up.

So I was very surprised to find groups of monks having chai or even cappuccinos in the cafés. In fact they were a common sight at Café One-Two near the Dalai Lama's monastery. They brought laptops into the café and would crowd around the screen, chatting away animatedly. Even more intriguing was the number of monks who had long conversations on their mobiles. Who could they be talking to?

I had the feeling that hanging around in cafés drinking cappuccinos probably wasn't expected behaviour for a monk, and this was confirmed when I heard the Dalai Lama talking on Tibet TV one night. His Holiness was clearly concerned that some monks and nuns were not showing enough devotion to the Dharma, and had possibly entered monastic life for the wrong reasons.

The Dalai Lama actually has a really progressive attitude to science and technology. He encourages bright young monastics to study Western science, and initiated the annual *Mind and Life* discussions between scientists and Buddhists in Dharamshala. These unique gatherings are aimed at fostering understanding between scientific thought and the Buddhist world view on subjects such as biology, physics and the workings of the brain.

The monks in the cafés certainly seemed to be all in favour of modern technology, but perhaps not quite in the way the Dalai Lama had in mind.

One of my motivations in learning Tibetan was to find out just what on earth the monks in the cafés were talking about. Sadly, all my eavesdropping was in vain, because I never became proficient enough at spoken Tibetan to understand what they were saying.

The best 'monk moment' of all came during Tibet Charity's end-of-year certificate ceremony. Each class had to present a short entertainment. For me the uncontested highlight of the day was Norbu's beginner class, all monks, standing in a semicircle and belting out the Bob Marley number *Three Little Birds*. "Don't worry about a thing, 'cause ev'ry little thing gonna be alright..." [2]

In my wildest fantasies I never imagined I would find myself in India watching a group of Tibetan monks doing reggae.

---

[2] *Three Little Birds* by Bob Marley and The Wailers, from their album *Exodus.* Island Records UK, 1977.

# Chapter Eleven

# *Walking the kora*

There were three ways of getting to town from Snow Height. The most straightforward method was to walk up Temple Road. The drawbacks were the steep climb, the uneven surface, having to avoid wandering cows and the occasional fresh cowpat, and of course the traffic.

Temple Road was meant to be one way downhill, while the uphill traffic took the steeper Jogiwara Road. However you needed to be alert because motorcycles and even cars used to regularly drive *up* Temple Road. Many of the motorcyclists also used to turn their engines off and coast silently downhill, so at dusk or after dark pedestrians had to be particularly careful on the road, and a good torch was an essential accessory.

It was an entertaining walk between Snow Height and town. Monkeys often gathered in the trees beside a small Hindu temple just up the road. I loved watching the baby monkeys playing and leaping fearlessly around in the trees, but it was best not to make eye contact with the adults who could be aggressive, hissing and baring their teeth. The monkeys were used to people and seemed quite sensible about traffic. Several times I saw an adult apparently watching for the road to be clear before the troop ran across.

It was a good place for bird watching, too. Raucous crows were everywhere, cawing and showing off. I once spotted a big black-shouldered kite sitting regally right at the top of a Himalayan cedar, like some sort of novel Christmas ornament. Another day, a sinister flock of hunch-backed vultures was flapping around above the forest. There were occasional pheasants and lots of small finch-like birds as well as the ubiquitous sparrows.

What with the animal life and the beautiful lined brown faces of the elderly Tibetans walking downhill to join the kora, there was plenty to look at.

If you felt more energetic or wanted to get to town in a hurry, you could use the goat path. This led straight up the steep hill behind Snow Height. It lived up to its name in being narrow, winding and quite tricky to negotiate. At first I found I had to have several stops 'to admire the view' on the way up. Eventually I could make it in one go, but still panting.

If you met another person on the goat path or even worse, a cow, it could be difficult to find a safe place to pass. Completing the obstacle course were tangles of half-buried water pipes sticking haphazardly out of the hillside.

The kora was the third way to town. It was definitely the most enjoyable but also the longest. To really appreciate it you needed to have time to spare and be in the right frame of mind, because the kora is the sacred path around the Dalai Lama's residence. It replicates the ancient Lingkhor path around the Potala Palace in Lhasa.

It is traditional in Tibetan Buddhism to circle stupas, temples and other sacred places in a clockwise direction, saying prayers for the cessation of suffering and the happiness of all living beings. In old Tibet, the Lingkhor - the path around the home of the Dalai Lama - was crowded with pilgrims praying and meditating as they trudged along the route. If they were really devout, they would cover its eight kilometre length in repeated prostrations.

The kora in McLeod Ganj is like a miniature version of the Lingkhor. The way is lined with white painted rocks, and the Himalayan cedars and oaks on either side of the path are hung with hundreds of prayer flags in all sizes and degrees of fadedness.

Beside the path are multicoloured mani stones carved with *Om Mani Padme Hum*, the mantra of the Bodhisattva of Compassion, of whom the Dalai Lama is the living incarnation. At intervals there are prayer wheels - twenty in a row, or a few together, and two huge ones which ring a bell when they get up enough momentum.

Most of the Tibetans walking the kora carry their own prayer wheels or prayer beads. They chant mantras as they go, but there's also a casual feel to the walk. People greet each other, stop for a chat, or rest on the benches placed at intervals beside the path. There are stunning views across to the mountains. Walking the kora feels like a very practical, everyday sort of devotion.

After a while, the path passes a gate leading to an old people's home, with *May all sentient beings be happy* painted on the wall beside the entrance. Then you emerge into a small open temple area. Clouds of incense waft across to a line of prayer wheels below two imposing stupas set in gardens of flowers. Early one morning I came across Ani-la, my Tibetan teacher, weeding in the garden by one of the stupas and looking very contented.

You pass the temple and circle three times around two huge prayer wheels, then continue up the hill past a beautiful and expensive guesthouse, and an open stone shelter housing a family of beggars.

At last you reach the end of the kora, framed on a clear day by a view of the towering Dhauladhar mountain range, and approach the entrance to the main temple complex. Here you're jolted back into the bustling life of the town: beggars, street sellers, insistent taxi drivers touting noisily for business, tourists taking photos, cows and crows, dogs and the occasional monkey.

Entering through the modest gateway under the *Where is the Panchen Lama?* sign, you go past the small museum and a couple of craft and book shops and up the steps to the temple itself, pausing - if you're a foreigner - for a cursory bag search by the security guards.

I never saw anyone prostrating on the kora itself, but on the upper terrace of the temple grounds is an area set aside for this demonstration of reverence for the three jewels of Buddhism, the Buddha, the Dharma and the Sangha. People fold their hands in prayer at the head, throat and heart, then measure their length on the floor - and repeat. I tried it (in my room) and found ten were exhausting, yet devout Buddhists, including elderly people, regularly complete thousands of prostrations.

When I walked the kora I felt as if I should be saying some sort of mantra to get into the spirit of the walk, so I began with "Om Mani Padme Hum." I felt a bit embarrassed repeating this mantra, even silently, because I really didn't understand it. I only knew it loosely translated as "Behold the jewel in the lotus," referring to the Buddha, and each syllable represented an aspect of compassion. I later learned that hundreds of pages have been written about the finer points of *Om Mani Padme Hum,* so I didn't feel quite so alone in my confusion.

"May all sentient beings be happy" felt like a good, positive thought to repeat. Sometimes I alternated with "May Tibet be free." This became "May Tibet be free in the Dalai Lama's lifetime," and finally as the implications of reincarnation started to sink in, "May Tibet be free in the Dalai Lama's *current* lifetime," which seemed to cover all the bases.

I found it really fascinating to be in a Buddhist town where religion was so much a part of daily life. The maroon-robed monks and nuns around town, the old people with their prayer wheels, waking every day to the faint sound of chanting by the monks in the monastery up the hill; all became a familiar part of the everyday scene.

Life in Dharamshala was full of surprises and unexpected events. One afternoon I came across a work gang of young nuns helping to clear debris from a building site next to their nunnery in Jogiwara Road. They were all laughing and chattering away while passing chunks of rubble from hand to hand.

That evening, as I walked back down the road, they were practising debating. I could hear the ritualised hand slapping and stamping which is used to emphasise a point as their clear voices drifted out through the twilight.

*Chapter Twelve*

# Listening to the Dalai Lama

I made my first visit to the Dalai Lama's temple a few days after I arrived in Dharamshala, and laid a khata in front of the photo of His Holiness as a mark of respect. I'd been given it in New Zealand several years before while working for the Lake Taupo Arts Festival. As part of the Festival programme a group of Tibetan monks had made a sand mandala. It felt very satisfying to return the khata to its source, as it were.

I had barely settled into a teaching routine when we had a week's holiday. Mahatma Gandhi's birthday was followed by several days of teachings by the Dalai Lama. These events brought a rush of tourists to Dharamshala. Many Indians came to the hills for a few days' vacation around Gandhi's birthday, and several thousand Russian Buddhists descended on the town for the teachings at the Dalai Lama's temple.

McLeod Ganj became a kaleidoscope of colourful costumes and interesting faces. Many of the Russians were of Mongolian origin and came from Kalmykia in the far east of Russia, near the Caspian Sea. The women dressed up for the teachings in beautiful traditional brocade gowns, and a number of the men wore long-sleeved tunics and little round hats with gleaming silver points on top. It was like a glimpse into the court of Kublai Khan.

I saw elderly Russians who could have stepped straight out of the pages of a Tolstoy novel, with long white beards and embroidered full sleeved shirts, belted over baggy trousers tucked into knee boots. Among the crowds, the Indian women gleamed in their gorgeous saris and gold jewellery. The Tibetan women who attended the teachings often wore their best turquoise, silver and coral necklaces, and many Tibetan

50

men, who usually dressed in Western clothes, had donned their traditional chuba.

I attended two sessions of His Holiness' teachings, well aware of my ignorance about Buddhism, but eager not to miss the experience which was clearly a high point of life in Dharamshala. I took along a cushion and a cheap FM radio to catch the English translation of the talks, but left my mobile phone and camera behind as they were forbidden in the temple grounds during the teachings.

I arrived with about half an hour to spare and joined a queue of foreigners. We all had our bags searched and were frisked before entering the temple grounds. Security at the temple was usually quite relaxed, but during the teachings it was taken much more seriously.

The upper level of the temple was full of people by the time I got there. The Russians who sponsored the talks had the best places in the room where the Dalai Lama was going to sit. Next door was crowded with monks. Both these rooms contained beautiful bronze statues, murals and thangkas, and could normally be visited quite freely. Entry to the upper levels was only allowed during the teachings if you got a special pass, and it was very crowded. Hundreds of foreign Buddhists were crammed into any space they could find in the areas around the upper temple.

I was happy to set myself down near the back of the lower courtyard where most of the Tibetans were sitting. I found a good place under a tree, and the old monk sitting cross-legged next to me amused himself by watching as I did a few drawings of people in the crowd.

The gates to the Dalai Lama's residence opened promptly at nine o'clock. He emerged into the temple grounds, beaming as usual and striding out in front of a group of monks and bodyguards. As I had noticed when he drove by on the road, the Tibetans showed deep respect for him with folded hands and lowered eyes, while many of the Westerners craned to get a better view.

It took several minutes for His Holiness to reach the upper level of the temple, because he stopped frequently to acknowledge people in the crowd. When eventually the teaching started, his amplified voice boomed out in Tibetan and I fiddled with my FM radio to get the English translation. To my disappointment I found the translator's delivery quite monotonous and it was hard to concentrate on what he was saying. It didn't help that the tuner on the cheap radio was rather loose and it kept slipping into the Russian or German translations.

If I had been hoping for some deep Buddhist revelation I didn't get it - the whole experience was just too strange and unfamiliar. After a while I stopped trying to make any sense of what I was hearing and occupied myself by watching the crowd and doing a little sketching.

After about an hour, I noticed several young monks with enormous teapots climbing the stairs to the upper level. The Dalai Lama stopped talking and the translation also ceased. Suddenly a loud slurping noise came through my headphones. This was repeated over the next few minutes, then there was a pause and the interpreter's embarrassed voice asked, "Could you hear that?"

An American voice drawled, "Man, *everyone* could hear that!"

Tea was served to every area of the temple by a work gang of monks. It was Tibetan tea, milky with a slight salt taste and globules of fat on the surface. To my surprise, I found it really tasty. Rounds of Tibetan bread were also handed out, although the crowd was so big that not everyone was lucky enough to get the bread. Dipped in the tea, the light, spongy bread made a very filling snack.

The morning session of teachings ended at around noon when the Dalai Lama came down the steps to a black car, and was driven back into the grounds of his residence. The crowd in the courtyard left the temple grounds and I was carried along with the rest.

During the second session I attended, the Dalai Lama conducted an initiation. This ceremony takes Buddhists to a higher level of study. After the ritual, he quite sternly reminded the participants that just having taken part in the initiation was not enough, and they would need to study seriously every day to make it worthwhile.

I enjoyed the atmosphere of the teachings, but they were aimed at people who had far more understanding of Buddhism than I did. My growing appreciation of the Dalai Lama and his philosophy came from regularly watching His Holiness on Tibet TV. Many of the programmes were in Tibetan but they often showed talks recorded on his frequent European and American tours, when he spoke in English.

He often repeated similar themes - the power of compassion, the need for ethics in a secular society, gaining world peace through inner peace, practising forgiveness. I noticed that when he spoke to foreign audiences the Dalai Lama often joked or laughed, but his talks to the Tibetans were much more intense and serious.

Two of his stories made a deep impression on me, and one changed my behaviour and has even saved lives.

In the first story he talked about a monk, "Quite an ordinary monk" who had been imprisoned by the Chinese in Tibet for many years. He was eventually released and made his way to India where he met the Dalai Lama. In the course of conversation, the monk said he had several times been in great danger. The Dalai Lama asked what kind of danger and he replied, "Danger of losing compassion for the Chinese."

The other story came out of a chance meeting between the Dalai Lama and a group of women during a stopover on a plane journey somewhere in India. One of the women swatted a mosquito. His Holiness was horrified - probably nobody had ever killed a living creature in front of him before. The Dalai Lama used this story to reinforce his message about compassion for all living beings. His own attitude to mosquitoes was that the first one is welcome to take some blood, the second not quite so welcome, and so on...

After hearing this story a couple of times I found myself tenderly putting unwelcome insects outside my room instead of thoughtlessly killing them. I removed a cockroach to the grassy bank beside the stairs and told it, "If you'd been in Taranaki, mate, you'd be dead!"

I even spared a wasp after it got tangled up in my shirt and stung me. Now that I am back in New Zealand, I don't kill cockroaches as I used to, and I try to stun flies and put them outside before they wake up.

"Thank the Dalai Lama," I tell them.

## Chapter Thirteen

# *"How is your puja going?"*

Dharamshala was a magnet for tourists even when the Dalai Lama wasn't teaching. They went trekking, studied Buddhist philosophy, went to yoga classes and took part in meditation retreats. Some did some volunteer work to help the Tibetan cause, while others were happy just to hang out and soak up the atmosphere of Little Lhasa. People who had spent time travelling around India often said they found the pace of life in Dharamshala much more relaxed than in other places.

The climate was certainly less extreme than on the plains or further south. The monsoon had just finished when I arrived in late September. Over the next few weeks we had several terrific downpours with exciting crashes of thunder rumbling round the mountains, then it was fine, pleasantly warm and perfectly windless until mid-November when the temperature began to fall a little.

Many of the visitors to Dharamshala were Buddhist converts, and people often assumed I was a Buddhist as well. One Indian man who attended the philosophy lectures next door to our Tibetan class used to regularly confuse me with someone else, and would inquire sympathetically, "How is your puja going?"

The majority of the foreign Buddhist converts had a look of aging hippies, festooned with shawls and prayer beads. They tended to exude a slightly off-putting air of sombre earnestness, in contrast to the Tibetans whose approach to their religion was cheerfully matter-of-fact.

I sometimes detected a kind of competitiveness among the foreigners, almost as if there was a virtue in being more Buddhist than anyone else. I listened with irritated fascination one day in Café One-Two as a Frenchman and an Italian sparred with each other:

"My geshe said I *had* to come here and seek refuge with the Dalai Lama," against, "I went to a blessing by the Karmapa and at the end, you know, I felt this strong pull to approach him, so I went up to him and he ..." and so on.

However, my prejudice about foreign Buddhists was seriously challenged when I encountered Ron. He was from the north of England and moved in to Snow Height shortly after I arrived. The word went around that he spent months every year in Dharamshala and always rented the same room.

When I first met Ron, I couldn't work him out at all. He was in his fifties, short, muscled and with a big beer belly. Several of his front teeth were missing. He drank Kingfisher beer in vast amounts, had a jolly laugh and talked enthusiastically about English football and rock music. He looked as if he would be more at home in a long distance lorry than on the streets of Dharamshala.

It turned out that Ron was a Buddhist from way back, long before it became fashionable in the West. From his teens he'd been working for the Tibetan cause, and his knowledge of Tibetan history and Buddhist philosophy was formidable. He had meditated in remote monasteries, and was married to a Tibetan woman he had met in Dharamshala during the seventies. He'd been coming back to McLo for years and knew everyone - in fact he'd outlasted many of his Tibetan friends who had moved on to other countries.

While foreign Buddhists of Ron's calibre seemed to be outnumbered by the aging hippies, meeting him gave me a useful wake up call about jumping to conclusions.

Just before Fleur left, in tears, for her job interview in Japan, two new teachers arrived at Tibet Charity.

Naomi and John were originally Scottish but now lived in Wellington. They were civil servants who had taken a TESOL course so they could teach English overseas in their holidays, and had previously worked in Italy, China and Lithuania. Their arrival was perfectly timed, as John was able to slot straight into teaching Fleur's class while Naomi took a study group in the afternoons.

Another new arrival was Jen, a young vet from England. Despite looking as if she had barely left school, she was fully qualified and very enthusiastic about taking part in the annual job of catching, sterilising and vaccinating the local stray dogs.

She was also terrifically impressed with a huge, docile bull which used to wander around town, nosing into rubbish skips and gazing mournfully through the doors of cafés.

"I'd love to get my hands on those testicles," Jen would chortle.

Ron was a big fan of drinks parties in the roof garden of Asian Plaza, one of the few restaurants in town where you could buy alcohol. The conversation was lively and varied when we all gathered round the table to drink our Kingfishers and watch the sun sink over the mountains.

*Chapter Fourteen*

# Two monasteries, a school and a noodle factory

Not long after I arrived at Tibet Charity, the volunteer teachers were taken on a special day trip by the Director. We piled into a large taxi and drove down the narrow winding road, past the Central Tibetan Administration complex and the Tibetan hospital with its special clinic for torture victims. We dodged the early morning traffic coming up the hill, weaved our way through the congested shopping centre of lower Dharamshala and finally made it out into the countryside.

The road wound downward through small villages where people were heading into the fields to work, and children in spotless uniforms were walking to school. The monsoon rains had left the countryside looking fresh and lush.

Kangra is a famous tea-growing region. As we started climbing again, we passed through acres of low dark green hedges which the Director identified as tea bushes. We were now about 500 metres lower than Dharamshala and the countryside was quite different - fertile, often terraced and more intensively farmed than higher in the mountains.

The villages we passed through also seemed a little more prosperous. The Tibetan atmosphere of McLeod Ganj was completely missing here - these were Indian villages, each with its Hindu temples and shrines. At one point we slowed down outside a small town and the Director pointed out a zoo where a few brown bears were sleeping in the shade.

In other ways the countryside was still quite wild, despite India's millennia of habitation. The narrow winding road skirted rushing rivers with gigantic boulders brought down by the monsoon rains. On the verges sat little groups of monkeys.

Some were engrossed in grooming one other while others gazed thoughtfully at us as we passed.

It took us nearly two hours to get to our first stop, the Central Tibetan School in Chauntra. Our Director was its first headmaster and makes regular visits with groups of volunteers from Tibet Charity.

We arrived just in time for assembly. The whole school was lined up in rows outside the main building. There were around three hundred and sixty children, ranging in age from six to sixteen. They all had their hands inspected for cleanliness and chanted the mantra of Manjushri, the Bodhisattva of Wisdom. They finished off with a rousing version of the Tibetan national anthem, accompanied by a large band of drums and flutes. Nearly a quarter of the school seemed to be in the band.

As the children dispersed noisily in all directions we were shown into the Headmaster's office where we were intrigued to see a large electric prayer wheel whirling away.

After a welcome cup of chai and fried biscuits we were taken on a tour of the school. Our first stop was the library, which was decorated with beautiful thangkas and seemed well stocked with books in a number of languages. On a table was a small elderly computer similar to one I owned twenty years ago.

In the science lab there were shelves of pipettes and beakers as well as student projects in English about Einstein, Edward Jenner, Isaac Newton and other scientific heroes, a large painting showing *Binary Fission in Amoeba*, jars of preserved starfish and snakes, and various plants at different stages of growth. The solid wooden benches and basic equipment made me think of science class during my own schooldays in the sixties.

The dormitories were spartan and extremely tidy, with folded blankets and pillows piled at the head of each bunk, a shelf full of shiny metal mugs and a small shrine with pictures of the Buddha, the Karmapa and the Dalai Lama. A sign on the wall read *Do not clean ur hand and shoes on curtain.* The children's shoes were arranged neatly in racks and their padlocked metal trunks were piled in the hallway near the long white tiled wash basin.

When we visited some of the classrooms we were all impressed by how polite and well behaved the children were. They seemed a little shy, but that's only to be expected when several large foreigners suddenly march unannounced into your classroom.

We were interested to read the daily timetable on the wall outside one of the classrooms. The children get up at 5.15am, and their day had already included washing, yoga, breakfast, prayer and study, all before we had seen them at assembly.

From the six-year-olds in the Montessori class to the senior students practising their debating techniques, the school was humming along quietly. We looked into the hall which was decorated with murals of Tibet, two fine painted dragons and a portrait of the Dalai Lama. A music class was in progress. The instruments included flutes, long-necked stringed instruments and a kind of dulcimer.

The students performed a couple of traditional songs and dances, as well as two songs about His Holiness. One had been composed to celebrate the Nobel Peace Prize which he was awarded in 1989, much to the disgust of the Chinese government which portrays him as a dangerous 'splittist.'

Steam and delicious smells were issuing from the kitchen, where huge pots of dahl and rice were being prepared for the school lunch. However, we had another visit to make before our own lunch break.

Not far from the school was the Dzongsar Institute. This modern monastery was an impressive collection of three-storeyed buildings surrounded by gardens, stupas, tiled walkways and lawns bordered by neatly trimmed hedges. The grass had clearly got out of hand and a couple of Indian women were cutting it back with scythes. The Institute houses five hundred monks and looked like a very comfortable place to spend years of study.

Chalked on the pavement as we walked through the grounds were the eight auspicious symbols of Buddhism - the pair of fish, vase, lotus, conch shell, wheel, parasol, endless knot and victory banner. I'd also seen these painted on the driveway by the Dalai Lama's temple. The Director told us that the auspicious symbols represent different aspects of the Buddha's teachings.

The Dzongsar site was dominated by the temple, a massive square building in muted pink with gold trimmings, surmounted by the Dharma wheel flanked by two deer. We walked up the imposing flight of stairs and examined the painted façade. It was a riot of bright colours and painstaking detail, with landscapes, deities, geometric designs and auspicious symbols all vying for space. I recognised the wheel of life from the Tibet Library in Dharamshala, held up by a dark and scowling monster.

Inside, the temple was vast and sumptuous. The only other Buddhist temple I had visited was the Tsuglag Khang at the Dalai Lama's monastery. Although it was bright and somewhat cluttered, it seemed a paragon of modesty and restraint compared to the Dzongsar temple.

There was a huge seated golden Buddha flanked by hundreds of smaller statuettes, a tall standing Buddha, multi-coloured hangings, huge thangkas, flowers, painted pillars topped with demons' heads - it was hard to take it all in. The monastery was inaugurated in 2007 and everything was shiny and new. The low platforms where the monks sit were quite plain, but I thought it would be very easy to get distracted from your meditation in surroundings like these.

Back in the taxi, we bumped our way over the dirt road from the Dzongsar Institute to Bir. This small village is renowned as the filming location for *The Cup,* a charming, funny movie about a football-crazy young novice monk scheming to watch the World Cup final.

Bir is also a famous centre for paragliding. In fact, as we sat in a tiny restaurant waiting for our lunchtime momos, we spotted a paraglider sailing over the hills above the town. Draped over the forest canopy we could see a colourful smudge which looked suspiciously like the sail of a wrecked glider.

After lunch we crossed the road to a series of mostly disused buildings. These had formerly housed craft workshops where hand-woven Tibetan carpets were made, but they were no longer in use because the workers couldn't make enough money from the carpet making. I thought about Trade Aid, the Fair Trade organisation I work for in New Zealand, and wondered if the workers had been able to negotiate fair prices for their carpets. If they had, the workshops might still have been functioning.

One of the buildings was being used as a noodle factory. The Director was keen to buy some freshly made noodles, so we made our way past a cow dozing under a string of prayer flags and peered into the dimly lit factory.

There's something fascinating about watching waves of noodle dough flowing out of a machine, and in the corner the final product was slung over row upon row of drying racks. The Director bought several packets of noodles coiled and neatly wrapped in newspaper, and stowed them away carefully in the boot of the taxi.

As we drove out of town, we paused by a couple of SUVs bearing the insignia of a paragliding company. The smudge of colour we had seen in the hills was indeed a crashed paraglider, but the pilot was uninjured and the team was just setting off to rescue him. It looked like a long trek through the forest. I suppose if you're a paraglider in the Himalayas, the possibility of coming down in uncomfortable territory is just part of the deal. Maybe it adds to the excitement. We all agreed that our preference was to keep our feet on the ground.

The road now became a very winding riverside track through a beautiful forest of Himalayan oaks and cedars. We passed a couple of men with donkeys, and held our breath as the driver negotiated some slips where much of the road had disappeared alarmingly into the river. We also met a bus, luckily in a place with room to pass, but I wondered how it was going to get around the slips.

Eventually we drew into the courtyard of yet another imposing monastery, Sherab Ling, its dark red walls faced in white and its golden roof glinting in the sun.

We walked through a large vestibule about the size of a basketball court to reach the temple, which was inside the monastery building. A few monks' robes were slung over the railings around the perimeter of the entrance hall, giving the place a reassuringly domestic feel.

The entry to the temple itself was even more imposing than at the Dzongsar Institute. Large golden Chinese style lions flanked the staircase, the painted pillars were wound around with multi-coloured dragons, and the interior of the temple was so cluttered with decoration it was quite claustrophobic. The walls were painted a deep rich crimson, but they could hardly be seen through the mass of thangkas, decorated pillars, multi-coloured fabric hangings like enormous windsocks, low slung lamps and lots of gold tracery. The theme seemed to be, "If there's a plain patch of wall, ceiling or floor, cover it!"

Elaborately framed portraits of both the Dalai Lama and the Karmapa were on display, and the Director told us the monastery belonged to the Kagyu school of Buddhism.

There are four main schools of Tibetan Buddhism: Nyingma, Kagyu, Sakya and Gelug. Each offers a different approach to the study and practice of Buddhism. The Dalai Lama's Gelug school places great emphasis on monastic discipline and sound scholarship. The Karmapa heads the Kagyu school which is renowned for its meditational techniques.

The visual excess in the temple was quite overwhelming, and we were glad to get outside again. In all this time we had set eyes on perhaps half a dozen monks, although the monastery houses several hundred monks and nuns. We could hear the distant sound of drums and trumpets, but the tune repeated so regularly we decided it was probably a recording. It gave the visit a slightly surreal feeling.

We got back into the taxi, drove for a few minutes, passed a row of beautiful white stupas, and parked outside the gateway of the monastery's retreat house and woodcraft studios.

Sherab Ling monastery lies near a main route but is relatively isolated in the forest, so it is a popular destination for people going on a meditational retreat. The guesthouse was located directly behind the monastery, separated from it by a shallow gully, and looked simple but comfortable.

We skirted a pair of sleeping dogs and ordered chai at the rudimentary teashop. While we were waiting we peered inside the woodcraft studio, where two carvers were creating delicate and convoluted dragon figures.

Throughout our tea break we could see an elderly Tibetan woman trudging round and round the nearest stupa with her prayer wheel. As we drove away on our two-hour journey back to Dharamshala she gave us a sweet, serene smile and raised her hand in farewell.

# Chapter Fifteen

# *"May all sentient beings be happy."*

I was curious to know more about the opulent Dzongsar Institute, so I checked it out on the internet. I was surprised to find that the author of the book I was currently reading was its Director, Dzongsar Jamyang Khentse Rimpoche. I'd picked up *What makes you not a Buddhist* in one of McLo's Buddhist bookshops. It offered a reasonably straightforward introduction to a complicated and intriguing subject.

I found that, unlike Christianity, faith is not a primary requirement of Buddhism. On the contrary, Buddha clearly told his disciples *not* to take his teachings as gospel truth, saying, "Just as gold is tested through burning, cutting and rubbing, likewise examine my words thoroughly, and only then accept them, not merely out of respect for me."

It made Buddhism seem like hard work. So much meditation, questioning and studying. No wonder the foreign Buddhists were so earnest. It seemed there was no easy ride on the Dharma road.

As I stumbled my way through *What makes you not a Buddhist* I started to get a few hazy inklings about the philosophical basis to Buddhism, although I had trouble with some of the most fundamental concepts. I thought long and hard about ideas like 'emptiness' and 'dependent origination' but found them really difficult to grasp.

Then again, I could see *practical* Buddhism in action every day in McLo. It was the old women and men circling the Library with their mantras and prayer wheels, the people walking the kora, my fun-loving students who had trekked over the mountains to be near the Dalai Lama, the monks chanting before dawn and the young nuns practising debating on the balcony of their nunnery.

Before I went to Dharamshala I was almost as ignorant about Tibet and the Tibetans as I was about Buddhism. I did know that, despite decades of exile from Tibet and oppression within it, with very few exceptions the Tibetan people have never resorted to violence; nor do they seem to harbour any hatred against the Chinese. This is so unusual in the modern world that it made me really curious to find out what made these people tick.

By the time we went on our outing, I'd read enough about Tibetan history to know that this positive attitude in the face of oppression is deliberate, not some unusual genetic trait in the Tibetan people. As with all societies, Tibetan history has had its share of crime, brutality and inequality. Despite what romantic foreigners might want to believe, Tibet was never Shangri-La.

The more I got to know the Tibetans, the more they impressed me. Yes, temples such as Dzongsar and Sherab Ling are opulent, but individuals live very modestly. Even the Dalai Lama lives the life of a simple monk.

Despite their exile, their precarious existence as refugees and their economic poverty, the Tibetans struck me as robust people - emotionally strong, resilient and quick to laugh; optimistic and willing to make the best of whatever life throws at them.

Walking the kora with the Tibetans and thinking about the implications of "May all sentient beings be happy" was turning out to be strangely liberating. I began to feel my mind opening out to encompass all the creatures of the earth, humans included, all alike in their underlying goal - to avoid suffering and experience happiness. I started to understand that the fluttering prayer flags and turning prayer wheels were a real and powerful expression of the amazing generosity of Tibetan Buddhism, and that everyone around me on the kora was genuinely imbued with that belief.

Each morning as I ate breakfast on my balcony, I would watch the old people coming up the road to walk the kora. One very elderly lady used to pause frequently and bend over on the path. Eventually I realised she was picking up worms or insects and putting them tenderly into the grass.

I gradually began to understand how much Buddhism is an integral part of the Tibetans' existence. "May all sentient beings be happy" is not just a mantra, it's a way of life.

*Chapter Sixteen*

# *The Man in the Box*

One of the most poignant examples of community compassion only really came to my attention several months after I had left India. This was the story of the Man in the Box.

I was walking through town one day with Lindy not long after I first arrived in McLo, when she said, "See that box over there? Did you know there's a man living in it?"

We both stared at the box. It was metal, about the size of a large packing case, and raised on legs about half a metre above the ground. The open side facing the street was hung with a grimy cloth. Behind it I could dimly make out a shape lurking in the gloom.

"Is he a beggar?" I asked.

Lindy said she had never seen the man begging; in fact she had hardly seen him at all. Someone had told her that he had lived in the box for many years, and that local people gave him food. He never spoke and only occasionally left the box to relieve himself in the street.

We often used to pass that way as we walked through town, but the Man in the Box never intruded on our lives. He didn't actively beg and spent most of his time inside the box, so it was easy to forget that someone was actually living in the squalid metal container in the heart of McLo's shopping centre.

The health of the Man in the Box apparently took a turn for the worse during December 2010, after we had left town. The Tibet Charity nurses stepped in and started treating a number of painful sores caused by his incontinence. They persisted in looking after the man for several months, but his condition deteriorated to the point where eventually in June 2011 he had to be taken to hospital. Even then he made it clear that he wanted to go back to his box, which is probably the only place he felt safe. A few days later, that is where he died.

After his death, the story of the Man in the Box was reported in *The Wall Street Journal*, of all places.[3]

It seemed that nothing was known about him. He may have been Indian or perhaps Pakistani. All anyone knew was that he had arrived in McLo as a teenager some time in the 1960s. He had been seen with a woman, but when she left town he stayed behind. He had taken refuge in the box outside an Indian restaurant, and it was the restaurant owners who first started feeding him.

For over forty years - almost the entire span of the Tibetans' life in exile - the Indians and Tibetans in McLo looked after The Man in the Box. They gave him clothes, bedding, food and cigarettes, even though he never spoke or tried to make human contact. It sounds as if he was autistic.

In New Zealand, The Man in the Box would have been reported to some government agency and taken into official care. In India, most people don't have that option, and it falls back on the community to do what they can with limited resources. However, any system has its flaws - in New Zealand it was recently reported that an old man who died in a council flat was only discovered a year later. I wonder if that would happen in India.

To be honest, when I was in McLo I never really gave the Man in the Box much thought. He was just another aspect of a strange new environment that I gradually became accustomed to, like the roaming cows, the monkeys, or the old Indian woman with no fingers who had to sit on the side of the road and beg for a living.

However, in the eyes of the Tibetans, The Man in the Box was a sentient being who, like themselves, was trying to escape the cycle of suffering and achieve happiness. They

---

[3] Stancati, Margherita. *Dharamsala's 'Man in the Box' Dies*.
The Wall Street Journal, 28 June 2011

knew he deserved their compassion, and through all the long years that is what they gave him.

*Bhagsu Road, McLeod Ganj. The scene of many traffic jams.*

*Two young Tibetans - two different ways of life.*

71

*Magnificent Buddha, Dzongsar Institute, Chauntra.*

*Work gang of nuns on a building site, Jogiwara Road.*

*The beauty and tranquillity of Norbulingka.*

*Yellow-billed blue magpie, Norbulingka.*

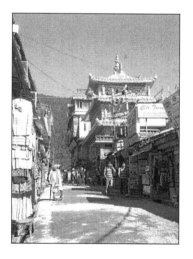

*A quiet moment in McLo's main street.*

*Jogiwara village with Triund plateau in the distance.*

*Nek Chand Rock Garden, Chandigarh.*

# Chapter Seventeen

# The Tibetan Children's Village turns fifty

Thousands of monasteries used to be the chief providers of education in Tibet, although there were a few secular community schools. Most families sent at least one child to be educated in a monastery, and up to a third of the population became monks or nuns.

Chinese government policy now regulates the education system, and reportedly favours Chinese students over Tibetans. Most of my students came from Amdo, where many children get no more than about three years' schooling. This is partly because their families are nomads and often on the move, but also because it is an isolated area and there aren't many schools available.

The Tibetans in exile have made a real effort to give their children a good education, and the results have been outstanding. These days many parents in Tibet send their children over the mountains to India to get a thorough grounding in Tibetan language, religion and culture, because it is no longer available in their own country.

We were fortunate enough to be invited to the fiftieth anniversary of the founding of the Tibetan Children's Village (TCV) schools.

These schools have an interesting and heart-warming history. In 1959, many Tibetans followed the Dalai Lama into exile in India. They found themselves in a desperate situation. The refugees were set to work on road gangs and lived in primitive conditions in tents, struggling to cope in an alien climate with unfamiliar food. Parents couldn't care for their children properly and many became ill.

The Dalai Lama arranged for the smallest children to be brought to Dharamshala, where a nursery was established and run by his sister, Tsering Dolma. Within a very short time she and her voluntary helpers, some of whom were women whose own children had died, had over eight hundred tiny children in their care. In 1964 Tsering Dolma died and the Dalai Lama's younger sister Jetsun Pema took over.

At first the children were sent to local day schools, but gradually the idea of a residential school took root, and became the pattern for the ongoing development of TCV. The children live with house parents in communal houses within the school grounds. They receive an education in Tibetan, Buddhism and Tibetan history, ethics, English, Hindi, mathematics, geography, world history and science.

Today there are around a dozen TCV residential and day schools in northern and southern India and Ladakh, as well as vocational training centres, youth hostels and the Dalai Lama Institute of Higher Learning in Bangalore. Over forty thousand children have gone through the Tibetan Children's Villages, and the current enrolment is around sixteen thousand, from nursery age to higher learning.

Tibetans love a celebration, and crowds of people gathered at TCV in upper Dharamshala for the fiftieth Jubilee. The hillsides around the dusty grassless football ground were dotted with monks, nuns, families, old people, colourful sun umbrellas and dogs. I spotted Jetsun Pema greeting students as they lined up to wait for His Holiness to arrive. She has retired from day-to-day duties but is still very much involved in TCV.

The Tibet Charity group had been allocated seats on the lower level of the main building, on the floor below where the Dalai Lama would sit. We found our places among a crowd of TCV's foreign sponsors and Tibetans in their traditional chubas.

I leafed through the Golden Jubilee booklet we had been given. There were photos and stories about many of TCV's former pupils, including Tibet Charity's head of nursing and one of the Dalai Lama's official interpreters (not the tea

76

slurper of the teachings.) All their personal stories emphasised the love and support they had received as children of TCV. Many had returned to the TCV schools to teach.

Another little booklet entitled *Metok* contained essays by current students. One girl talked about seeing her father beaten to death by soldiers on the day the family had their bags packed to leave Tibet. *What I make of my life will be a tribute to my father,* she wrote.

A boy in his last year of school marvelled at the stupendous change in his circumstances. He had gone from being an illiterate herd boy in a remote Tibetan village to an educated school leaver, with a wealth of possibilities ahead of him.

The TCV children were gathered excitedly in a grandstand to our left. They seemed to be all ages and sizes in their bright blue trousers and green shirts. The senior students were sumptuously dressed in the traditional costumes of Tibet's provinces, Kham, Amdo and U Tsang, with lots of brocade, fur hats and heavy jewellery.

The Dalai Lama's car rolled into the grounds and everyone in front of us stood up and craned to see him, so I caught just a momentary glimpse of his shaven head as he made his way up the stairs.

To open the day's festivities the school band did a march past, and the senior students sang the national anthems of India and Tibet. I noticed many of them gazing mesmerised in the direction of the balcony where His Holiness sat, directly above us.

The programme was a mix of colourful entertainment and excruciatingly long speeches. The Tibetan speakers seemed to go on forever and we were relieved to be diverted by a tiny woman with an enormous teapot, followed by a man with a plate of fried biscuits. Tibetan hospitality on these occasions is amazingly generous and well organised. When I watched the ceremony on TV some time later I saw that the whole crowd of several thousand had been served tea.

The speeches finally came to a welcome end. This was the cue for the horde of young children to race out onto the football pitch with their teachers. They lined up in ragged rows and performed a couple of enthusiastic action songs. This was followed by a large scale calisthenics display by the older students, culminating in the formation of *75* and *70*, the ages of the Dalai Lama and the much loved Jetsun Pema, known as Ama-la (Mother). The finale was presented by the students in costume, who performed a really lovely set of traditional songs and dances. The Dalai Lama apparently slipped away quietly before the end, and the rest of us joined the happy crowds making their way back to town.

On the second day of the celebrations, there was a performance of the Tibetan opera *Milarepa.* Naomi and I seemed to be the only ones in our group who were excited about this. Milarepa lived in the eleventh century and is considered one of Tibet's most outstanding yogis and poets.

His story sounded like a promising theme for the stage. Milarepa's father died when he was a boy, and his wicked uncle and aunt stole the family farm and forced the young Milarepa, his mother and his sister to be their slaves. At his mother's instigation, Milarepa left home and studied black magic under a famous sorcerer. He was obviously a good student, because he managed to call up a terrible hailstorm which killed thirty-five of his uncle and aunt's extended family.

Having taken his revenge in this dramatic fashion, Milarepa was racked with guilt and sought out the foremost Buddhist teacher of the day, Marpa the Translator. Marpa gave Milarepa a series of tasks to perform, building and then destroying a huge tower. Finally he agreed to teach him and the pupil excelled, attaining Vajradhara (enlightenment) in his own lifetime. Eventually Milarepa went up into the mountains where he meditated for years in a cave. He lived on a diet of nettles until his skin turned green, teaching a growing number of disciples and composing the inspiring poetry for which he is renowned throughout Tibet.

Naomi and I were particularly intrigued by the green skin aspect of the story and decided to go and see the opera.

Apparently it started early in the morning and went on all day. We caught an early tuk tuk and putt-putted our way out to TCV.

The opera had been going for about an hour when we arrived. A big crowd was gathered in front of a beautiful open canopy decorated with auspicious symbols and strings of prayer flags. We could see a papier mâché cave at the back of the stage.

We watched for about an hour. The opera was being performed by a professional group from TIPA and was very well done, as far as we could judge. It was both sung and spoken, and the plot was interspersed with songs, dances and a couple of comic routines. It was all very colourful and leisurely, and it appeared that the story itself had barely started. Milarepa spent some time deciding to leave home, had a touching farewell scene with his mother, and danced his way with several companions around the stage. The sorcerer came on with dramatic stampings and wild gestures.

Naomi and I looked at each other and calculated that at this rate Milarepa would be in his cave and turning green some time toward evening, so we decided to leave. We clearly lacked the patience of the Tibetan audience who were enjoying every minute of the show.

It had actually been a very interesting morning, not only seeing the opera but also observing the Tibetan crowd, including some of the TCV house mothers with broods of small children in tow.

This was not the end of my fascination with Milarepa. I bought a book about him with examples of his poetry, in which he exhorts his disciples and others to practise the Dharma.

I also noticed one day that a local café was screening a movie version of his story. Naomi and John were back in New Zealand by then, so I used the lure of the nettles and green skin to persuade Suzette to come with me. Sadly the pace of the film version was almost as slow as the opera and it was not as well acted, although with the traditional costumes and houses and the dramatic landscape, it was an interesting glimpse into old Tibet.

The film ended just after Milarepa completed his tasks for Marpa, so once again we missed out on seeing him eating nettles and turning green. But I had learned a lot about one of Tibet's greatest mystics.

# Chapter Eighteen

# *Norbulingka*

My birthday fell on a Saturday, and I decided to spend the day at Norbulingka, the Tibetan Centre for the Arts. This is where the visual arts of Tibet are preserved, and there are open workshops where you can see traditional thangka painting, printing, appliqué and tailoring, wood carving and metal craft.

Naomi, John, Suzette and I hired Snow Height's taxi for an hour's drive to Sidhpur, where we were dropped off at the elaborately decorated entrance to Norbulingka.

It was a stunning place to walk around. The Institute is based on the original Norbulingka Palace, the summer home of the Dalai Lama in Lhasa. We really appreciated the lovely, tranquil atmosphere after the jerry-built architecture and busy streets of McLeod Ganj.

The buildings were simple but elegant, with dragon-headed spoutings and bright multi-coloured pillars and eaves in the Tibetan style. There were clear pools of water overhung by lush greenery and beautifully maintained flower gardens. Groves of trees were set about with painted mani stones and hung with prayer flags. I spotted a yellow-billed blue magpie with a long black, white and light blue tail. It was the same type of bird I'd glimpsed on my first morning in Dharamshala, but this time I could admire its beautiful colouring up close.

We toured through the workshops watching the craftspeople and marvelling at the high quality of the work. In the metal workshop were huge beaten copper statues of the Buddha and various deities. There was a tremendous din and I was concerned to see that the workers wore no ear protection.

It was quieter in the woodwork section where the carved screens and pieces of furniture featured elephants, dragons and snow lions. They were immensely detailed and elaborate. Even more silent and concentrated was the atmosphere in the thangka workshop, where two rows of painters were working with super-fine brushes on mandala paintings and representations of the Buddha.

There was a small but beautiful temple in the grounds with a large golden Buddha and gorgeous multi-coloured murals and hangings. We also looked through a small doll museum which featured lively dioramas of traditional Tibetan life, including our old friend Milarepa the mystic in his cave.

The gift shop was a big step up from the street stalls of McLeod Ganj, both in the quality and price of the merchandise. I ended up buying a lovely set of simple screen-printed cards featuring Tibetans and yaks. One card showed a line of people plodding through the snow, and I was vividly reminded of my students' stories of their flight over the mountains.

We lingered for a long time over a delicious lunch in the restaurant, enjoying the food and the relaxed atmosphere, and then took a final walk around the gardens before heading out into the real world of India again.

We fought our way through a mass of competing taxi drivers outside Norbulingka and decided on a quiet guy standing on the edge of the crowd. When he started leading us to his car I noticed he had two extremely deformed club feet. However, he was an excellent driver and his car horn played a jolly little tune, a welcome change from the usual harsh tooting.

Our next stop was the Gyoto Ramoche Monastery, the current home of the seventeenth Karmapa, head of the Kagyu school of Buddhism. This school was started by Milarepa's teacher Marpa the Translator in the eleventh century.

The Karmapa is still young, only in his twenties. He was born in Tibet and was courted by the Chinese, appearing at various official functions. Gradually the Chinese began restricting his movements and his ability to communicate with his followers. At the age of fourteen he made a daring escape from Tibet, arriving in India with his close attendants.

There was quite a controversy following the Karmapa's escape, as the Indian government seemed to feel it was too easily accomplished and he could be a Chinese agent. For a long time he was a virtual prisoner, unable to travel within India or overseas. This has now been relaxed, although he is still not allowed to visit his home monastery at Rumtek in Sikkim, as it is disputed border territory with China.

The Karmapa holds a public audience and teaching session each Saturday at the Gyoto Ramoche Monastery. Lindy and Fleur had been to it and said that the security checks had been very rigorous.

We knew we had missed that day's audience because we had spent so long at Norbulingka, so we were surprised to see a large group of people waiting in the monastery garden. Someone told us the Karmapa was due to walk through the garden and bless the crowd. This seemed like a great opportunity to catch sight of him. There were no security checks and it all seemed very relaxed.

After a while we were all motioned to line up beside the path. The tall, good looking young Karmapa appeared with his retinue of monks and started to walk down the line. I noticed that many people were holding out khatas to be blessed. At the last moment I slipped off my beaded *Free Tibet* bracelet and held it out. As he passed me the Karmapa murmured, "Thank you."

I felt quite thrilled - not every birthday includes a blessing from a revered Incarnation!

*Chapter Nineteen*

# A trek to Triund and other outings

Life in Dharamshala was a daily keep fit regime. Every morning I would walk down to the Library for Tibetan classes and then puff my way back up the hill. Eventually I could make the uphill journey in about twenty minutes, and my thighs were the firmest they had ever been.

Usually I would go back to my room at Snow Height, but if I decided to continue up to town instead, the quickest but most challenging route was up Jogiwara Road. It was very steep, and you had to watch out for underpowered vehicles hauling their way up the hill. The drivers tended to be more concerned about keeping their vehicles moving than about whether they were about to hit a pedestrian.

It was worth making the effort to climb Jogiwara Road because of the spectacular mountain views. I was also intrigued by a strange, perpetually half-finished hotel called Hunted Hill House, perched forlornly near the top of the steepest part of the road.

Soon after passing Hunted Hill House, you came to an inviting selection of shops and cafés, a good excuse for pausing regularly. Children played and shouted on the roof of a nearby nursery school. The shoe-shine men sitting by the roadside eyed your footwear and solicited for business. One day I watched in fascination as an itinerant knife sharpener peddled away furiously on a bicycle whose back wheel was raised on a stand. The cycling motion turned his grinding wheel and bright sparks were shooting out in all directions.

There were also many opportunities to walk for pleasure in the area around Dharamshala. From the main square you could stroll up Tipa Road past the Performing Arts Centre to the

Indian village of Dharamkot, the chosen holiday destination of young Israelis. The hotel signs were all in Hebrew and in the cafés you could order felafel as well as Indian food.

Just up the hill from Dharamkot was the Tushita Centre, famous for its meditation classes and retreats. Nearby was a yoga school and a little further on was a sign for an Ashram. Dharamshala was full of opportunities to explore different types of self improvement.

John the Scottish Kiwi went to regular yoga classes, but the rest of us preferred to combine our exercise with eating. We would regularly trek to somewhere outside town and have a leisurely lunch in a café.

There were some favourite gastronomic walks. If you continued on through Dharamkot you came to a family home which had been converted into a small home stay and pizza restaurant. The Indian family served the best Italian pizzas I have ever eaten.

Another popular walk was to Bhagsu, the main destination for Indian tourists. The most chaotic and noisy traffic jams occurred in the first one hundred metres of the Bhagsu Road. It was barely wide enough to take one lane of traffic, but had to cope with a two-way stream of cars, buses, trucks, tuk tuks and motorbikes all jockeying for space. At times it seemed there couldn't possibly be any way out of the gridlock, but somehow the vehicles always managed to inch past each other eventually.

It was all done with the utmost patience. In fact, the only person I ever saw lose their cool in a traffic jam was Suzette, who found the tooting particularly irritating. One day we were picking our way through the usual mess of stalled traffic. The car just behind us had no more than half a metre of space, but the driver edged forward and tooted loudly. Instantly Suzette whirled round, struck the windscreen with her umbrella right in front of the driver's startled face and yelled, "Don't do that!" He reeled back and people stared. As we scurried away Suzette muttered, "I really shouldn't have done that," and gave an extra large donation to the next beggar she saw.

Once out of town it was a very pleasant walk down the road to Bhagsu. There were a few stalls beside the route, including that of a woman thangka painter who sold me a beautiful painted mandala.

The monks used to take their laundry to the Bhagsu river to wash, and you would often see them trudging along with big bundles on their shoulders, sometimes with a following of sweet-faced young novices.

One thing I found strange and never really understood, was that Indian tourists frequently asked for our photos. A group of young men or a family would stop us on the road, ask us where we came from and then suggest a photo with us. It seemed impolite to refuse, so we would grin away with our arms around a complete stranger's shoulders, then they would thank us and continue on their way. I used to wonder what story the people at home would be told about us, or if we ever ended up on someone's Facebook page.

Bhagsu was a dusty little village with a few decent sized hotels and a number of restaurants. Our favourite was the German Bakery. There seemed to be nothing particularly German about it and there were very few baked goods on the menu, but you could get excellent cheese omelets and a superb rice pudding. Our drink of choice was hot honey lemon ginger with lots of freshly grated ginger.

Bhagsu's narrow streets were home to a good range of Indian shops, prime places to buy Kashmir shawls and cotton blouses. Beyond the shops was a Hindu temple, a rather unhygienic-looking swimming pool and a path to the river and Bhagsu waterfall, another popular destination.

The monks would head off down to the river where they would do their laundry and spread their maroon robes over the rocks to dry. Many of the local people also used to wash their clothes in the river and often made it a family day out with a picnic.

Alternatively you could take the steep path up to the waterfall, a rushing torrent (especially in the weeks after the monsoon) which fell into a clear, freezing pool. On the day

Andy, Naomi and I went there, an intrepid Finn was swimming around in the pool, watched by a group of amused Indians and Tibetans. It was much more pleasant to sit on the sun-warmed stones and enjoy a cup of chai from the teashop, before strolling back down the hill to Bhagsu and McLeod Ganj.

The most demanding day trek from McLeod Ganj was to Triund, a plateau in the mountains at a height of just over 2800 metres. I could see Triund every day when I walked up from the Library, and it looked like a long hard climb. However, Naomi and John wanted to try it, so with Lindy and a couple of Tibet Charity's Danish board members who were visiting, we set off early one Saturday morning. Lindy had done the climb before, so she was our guide.

Early in the walk, our group was joined by another climber. An elderly black dog tagged onto the party just after we left McLo, and went all the way to the Triund plateau and back with us. This behaviour was very unusual, as most of the dogs in Dharamshala found it an effort even to turn over during the day - they saved their energy for barking with great enthusiasm at night. We wondered if the dog could be a reincarnated mountaineer.

We climbed up the road to Dharamkot and joined a track which wound its way up through the Himalayan cedars and rhododendrons to the small Galu Devi Hindu temple. Next door to the temple was a small teashop aptly named *Rest a While*. We'd been on the trail about an hour, had climbed about 400 metres and were ready for a hot drink. In the distance we could see the great mountain range glowing pink in the sun. A group of yoga students was saluting the new day on the flat roof of a nearby Ashram.

We set off again from *Rest a While* and followed the trail as it wound around the mountainside. We zigzagged our way upwards, occasionally looking back toward the ever-diminishing town of McLeod Ganj and the wide sweep of the Kangra Valley. The narrow track has been used for centuries by shepherds and mountain traders, and I could easily imagine heavily laden men and donkeys trudging over the route through the years. We met a group of chattering Indian women coming down, but otherwise we saw nobody for an hour.

Eventually we rounded a corner and the plateau of Triund loomed large above us, with the Dhauladhar range behind it standing out against the clear blue sky. In front of us the track curved around to where a ramshackle little building was nestled into the hillside - the second teashop. It was a welcome sight. What civilized trekking!

The teashop was doing great business and there was quite an international crowd enjoying the chai and the view. We sat in the warm sun, looking across the valley to a cluster of small stone buildings scattered around the mountainside. I thought they might be animal shelters, but someone said they were hermits' huts used by monks on retreat. Two colourful paragliders were lazily riding the air currents high above us.

When we left the teashop I was still feeling quite energetic, but the trail gradually got steeper, and an hour later when the third teashop came in view my legs were aching and my enthusiasm was beginning to wane. Naomi and I decided we would take a long tea break and make the final push to the plateau in our own time. We could see the path zigzagging up the steep wooded cliff face. The most challenging part of the trek was still to come. We watched the others moving on up the trail while we sat in the sun enjoying our chai and eating chocolate bars.

The dreamy peace was broken as down the path bounded a horde of about forty Indian school children who greeted us cheerfully and plonked themselves down around us. They all had packs and were carrying an assortment of drums, cooking pots and a huge wok.

"What country are you from?" they asked. "We are from Palampur. Take my picture!" They'd been to Triund for a school camp. Two days earlier there had been a spectacular thunderstorm with lightning crashing over the plateau, but despite this - or maybe because of it - they assured us they'd had a wonderful time. Aged around eleven or twelve, they were lively, cheeky and fun.

They begged us to sing to them so Naomi did "Head and shoulders knees and toes" and I gave them "The Teddy Bears' Picnic," thinking *If I have enough breath for this, I must have enough to get to the top.* After they had responded with "Hare Krishna" we waved goodbye and went on our way.

A small group of weary looking adults was seated nearby. "Are you the teachers?" we asked. "Parents," they said.

The last part of the trek took us about an hour. The track had fallen away in places so we had to scramble over rocks and up small banks. As we stood catching our breath, a train of heavily laden donkeys passed by, picking their way delicately up the path. Then at last we could see the lip of the plateau just ahead. A few more minutes and we were there! It was noon, so we had taken five hours to climb 1100 metres.

The Triund plateau was a gently sloping meadow, beyond which the mountains loomed magnificently over the landscape. Great birds of prey, eagles or kites, wheeled overhead. It felt like a place where humans were making their tiny mark but nature was in control.

People were lazing on groundsheets all over the plateau. A couple of makeshift tent teashops were doing good business. I ordered an omelet with my honey lemon ginger drink, but whether through tiredness or the effect of the altitude, I couldn't eat more than a couple of bites. Our faithful old doggy companion flopped down on the ground and enjoyed a welcome snack.

It's possible to continue climbing further up the plateau to a nearby peak and the Snow Line Café, but a light mist was starting to come down, and in any case we all felt we had done enough for one day. We had a brief rest and headed back down the track.

Trekkers sometimes stretch the Triund climb over two days and stay the night on the plateau. You can hire sleeping bags and tents and take plenty of time to enjoy the sunset and explore the area. As for us, we took four hours to pick our way down the mountain path, and by the time we arrived back in McLo I was exhausted.

The next day as I walked up the road from Tibetan class, wincing at my aching calves, I gazed up at the plateau far above and thought *I've been there!* It felt good.

# Chapter Twenty

# *How to avoid dowdy or slacking*

Food can become a major preoccupation when you're travelling. It can really make a difference to the success of a trip - where and what to eat, if you can identify it, how it tastes. Then there's the issue of whether it will agree with you, and how to cope if it doesn't.

I had anticipated that eating in India for three months would be a bit of a challenge, especially as I don't like very spicy food. I reassured myself that Dharamshala was a busy tourist centre. There would probably be a variety of places to eat, and the standard of hygiene should be higher than in more remote areas.

The first time I ate Tibetan food was in Delhi, when Nina the German Buddhist recommended spinach momos. They were tasty and filling and the powerful chilli sauce came on a little side dish, so I could limit my intake to an interesting spiciness rather than a stomach-churning blast of heat.

Once I got to Dharamshala, I relied on my fellow teachers to tell me about the best places to eat. They had already been in town for two months and had a few favourites. They also warned me away from a couple of restaurants which they'd abandoned after a round of Delhi belly.

The restaurant of choice when I arrived was Nick's Italian Kitchen in Bhagsu Road. The perpetually smiling Nick and his genial waiters were all Indian and the cashier was a Tibetan, but they really did serve very tasty Italian food. One of my favourite meals was mixed vegetables with mushrooms and garlic sauce, closely followed by spinach ravioli. It was also well worth leaving room for desserts at Nick's. His chocolate brownie with hot fudge sauce was superb and he baked a mean cheesecake.

Nick's was a vegetarian restaurant, in common with most of the eating places in McLo. I didn't really miss eating meat, but I probably would have gone vegetarian in any case after someone pointed out the primitive little hut where chickens were slaughtered, on the corner of Bhagsu and Tipa Roads.

Pizzas were a favourite in McLo and several restaurants served them. Opinion was divided among the foreigners about which places served the best pizza. I was a big fan of the Roquefort and walnut pizza at the Namgyal café beside the Dalai Lama's temple complex. Not only did it taste great, but it seemed so bizarre to be eating an Italian style pizza, containing fancy French cheese, while listening to Tibetan chanting in a Buddhist temple complex in the Indian Himalayas.

Namgyal café was quite tiny and was decorated with bank notes from many countries, as well as the ubiquitous photo of the Dalai Lama. You could browse through a collection of travellers' discarded paperbacks while waiting for your order. The café was used as a training site for young Tibetans learning the restaurant business and the service tended to vary a bit in quality and enthusiasm, but the food was always good.

Another restaurant with monastic connections was Shangri La in Jogiwara Road, run by the Gyudmed Tantric Monastery. It was a dimly lit little place with heavy wooden tables and a very cheap menu. One of the tastiest dishes was Veg Mongolian: light vegetarian rissoles in gravy. The service tended to be quite leisurely and the monk on the cash desk never seemed to have enough change, but it had a pleasant atmosphere. You were often entertained by monkeys leaping along the balconies of the nearby apartments, or walking lightly over the bundles of power lines slung between the buildings.

Ron the English Buddhist knew every restaurant intimately after his years in Dharamshala, and swore by the family-run pizza café in the hills near Dharamkhot. Once I had tasted their pizzas I had to agree they were the best. They were cooked in a real wood-fired pizza oven and were deliciously crisp and tasty. The meal was made all the better by the wonderful view out over the valley from the courtyard where we ate, and the colourful birds singing and flying around the garden.

One of the few places where I ate meat was Ashoka, a slightly more upmarket Indian restaurant. They did a wonderful chicken korma and a fabulous tandoori chicken, so I suppressed any thoughts about the chicken slaughter house and just enjoyed the food. And survived.

Traditional Tibetan cooking featured a lot of meat, particularly yak. This was not surprising since Tibet is so high up that most vegetables couldn't survive. When my student Lhamo invited Lindy and me to lunch one day she served two kinds of steamed momo - one with spinach and the other with mutton, the local substitute for yak.

They were deliciously succulent, much better than the restaurant momos. We congratulated Lhamo and she smiled modestly. Once upon a time in small town New Zealand, women who made feather-light scones and superb pavlovas were held in high esteem, and I got the impression that being a great momo maker earns you the same kind of respect in the Tibetan community.

Lindy, Suzette and I took the opportunity to learn some Tibetan cooking techniques when we went to a soup making lesson taken by Tashi at Sangye's Kitchen. The course took place in a tiny room in Jogiwara Road, near where I'd heard Jampa talking so eloquently about the 2008 protests in Tibet.

The cooking class was a much more light-hearted affair. A dozen of us from several countries crowded around Tashi's wooden table as he took us through the basics of making thentuk (flat noodles in soup), momos in soup, and thukpa (wide noodles made of egg dough) in soup.

As with most cooking techniques, what looks simple when done by an experienced cook can be laughable when produced by a beginner, and most of our momos and noodles looked distinctly odd. It didn't make any difference to the taste so we had a lot of fun, ate the results with great enthusiasm, and left clutching sheets of recipes to try at home.

Lindy, Suzette and I enjoyed the soup lesson so much that we signed up for another class. This time Tashi taught us how to make different types of steamed momo. We even made chocolate momos, a non-traditional but extremely yummy variation invented by Tashi.

When I first arrived in McLo, Suzette showed me round a couple of small grocery shops where you could choose from a range of breakfast foods. I settled on a box of Mango Nut Crunch, mainly because it made the most ambitious claims for my future health and well-being:

*…Mango Nut Crunch has been much appreciated and motivated the liking and love of maximum personalities of various spheres of life in the world. Mango Nut Crunch avoids dowdy or slacking & keeps one alert, smart, attractive, young, impressive, dominating and longevity… keeps a persons ever-ready to take up any task successfully any time of a day or night & provide outstanding results… boosts appetite an orderly healthy routine, maintain smart physique, stamina and sexual urge.*

How could anyone resist such a wonder food? Sadly, Mango Nut Crunch seemed to consist mainly of cornflakes, and it was not easy to locate either the mango or the nuts. What a let-down!

Whenever I got sick of Mango Nut Crunch and its fellow cereals (all similarly unexciting) I would go up to town for breakfast. Café One-Two was the nearest and served lovely fresh fruit and curd, and slices of toast with really tasty liquid golden honey.

There was another café called Coffeetalk further up the road which served very good tsampa porridge. Their cappuccinos were works of art, with delicately drawn teddy bears or *Free Tibet* and *Love Tibet* slogans traced in the foam.

Sitting in the cafés was a good way of observing the other foreigners and the monks, as well as keeping an eye on the colourful life in the street. I had lots of interesting chats with strangers, but I would also take my laptop to the WiFi cafés and catch up on my email, while eavesdropping on the conversations at neighbouring tables.

Life was engagingly public in the cafés. One afternoon I was Skyping with my son Adrian in Coffeetalk. I mentioned I'd seen part of an English football match on TV the previous night, but had changed channels at half time and missed the rest of the match. Adrian (in New Zealand) said he'd check the final score for me.

"Oh, we want to know who won that match," said a couple of young Indians pausing by my table, so Adrian gave the score to us all from 12,000 kilometres away.

Toward the end of my stay in Dharamshala I discovered a café where you could watch free DVDs every night. Lhamo's Croissant was in Bhagsu Road not far from Nick's Café, but for some reason nobody I knew had been there. Once I tried it I kicked myself for not visiting earlier. The place was clean and comfortable and they served excellent food, including fresh salads, pumpkin soup and delicious cakes. Their chocolate croissants would not have been out of place in a French bakery.

The DVDs were screened in a small room upstairs where you sat on cushions behind low carved glass-topped tables. This was where we saw the long-winded film *Milarepa,* which ended so frustratingly before he went meditating, ate nettles and turned green.

I also dragged Lindy and Suzette along to a screening of a much more satisfying movie. *Ten Questions for the Dalai Lama* is an independent film made by an American couple. It not only includes a very interesting interview with His Holiness, but the film maker also travelled into Ladakh, filming Tibetans in a harsh but stunningly beautiful landscape. The people live the kind of traditional life that must be very similar to that of the people of Tibet before the Chinese invaded, and life in Tibet changed forever.

# Chapter Twenty-one

# *Russians, cows, goats and the odd mongoose*

We were quite a cosmopolitan mix of people at Snow Height Apartments. The complex was made up of about twenty rooms, eight in the lower building where I lived and another block of smaller, cheaper rooms further up the hill. As well as the foreign teachers, there were a number of other people who were staying for several months, such as English Ron, a jolly Korean woman who was in my Tibetan class and a shy young Russian woman who used to come down the steps every morning with her baby in a backpack.

Jim was another long-term resident. He was a middle-aged American who walked with difficulty using a stick, and adored the three lean cats that hung around the apartments. None of the staff ever seemed to pay much attention to the cats but Jim made up for this neglect by feeding and petting them, and they treated his room as their home. Whenever I met Jim on the stairs our conversation was exclusively concerned with the cats, so I never discovered anything about his background or what had brought him to India.

This was the case with most people who passed through Snow Height or with whom you might strike up a conversation in a café. You would learn a little about where they came from or what they were doing in India, and then you would each go your separate ways. I used to speculate about how many fascinating untold stories there must be in a place like Dharamshala. It truly lives up to its name as a sanctuary, not only for the Tibetans but for travellers from all over the world - Buddhists, Hindus, scholars, people drawn by the lure of India or the Dalai Lama, people looking for spirituality and meaning in their lives, people on guided tours, Europeans and

Americans escaping from the materialism of the West, dedicated supporters of the Tibetan cause, people on pilgrimages, hippies, teachers, Dharma bums and wanderers.

As long-term tenants at Snow Height we lived pretty independent lives. We didn't have room service and only really needed the staff when a light bulb blew or the TV channels got out of synch. This tended to happen quite often after the regular power failures.

Although we got most of the supplies we needed from the grocery shops in town, we would buy extras such as bottled water, juice or biscuits from the tiny office-cum-shop where we paid our monthly rent to the manager. The shop provided a useful service for residents of the various apartment houses on Temple Road, as well as passers-by and the students at the school. It did a steady trade from morning until late evening, selling newspapers, water, snack food, soft drinks, soap, toilet paper and long-life milk. A TV above the fridge played a nonstop succession of soap operas or cricket matches. At night one of the staff would sleep in the shop on a stretcher which was carried back upstairs each morning.

When they weren't busy sweeping the paths or doing maintenance jobs, the three or four Indian men on the staff would sit for hours outside the shop, chatting or just staring at the view. Sometimes they would play badminton on the road. Nearly every day one of the men would wash the hotel's tiny white taxi. After a computer was installed, the manager spent most of his day playing video games.

The majority of the routine cleaning jobs were done by a very small man who ran up and down the stairs and swept the paths energetically every morning. He was also in charge of rubbish disposal. We used to separate out our plastic bottles. These were put in a huge sack and humped off up the road, presumably for recycling, but all the other rubbish was collected in bags beside the shop.

Every so often an ancient goatherd would come by with his flock of seven or eight goats, and encourage them to rummage through the rubbish bags for titbits while he chatted to the staff. When the bags got full, the little man would take them over the road and throw them down the bank.

There was rubbish collection of a sort in Dharamshala but there was also a tremendous amount of debris strewn around. Local people - both Indians and Tibetans - didn't seem to have any qualms about disposing of their rubbish all over the place, and the garbage in the big skips provided by the Tibetan administration often got raided by monkeys, goats, cows and people.

I was a bit surprised by this messy attitude. I had heard the Dalai Lama talking about restoring a clean environment to Tibet, and I thought his people might have made a bit more effort in their present surroundings. There *is* a local environmental group, a dedicated core of Tibetans and foreigners who regularly pick up rubbish, encourage recycling and promote the use of filtered instead of bottled water. They have managed to have plastic bags banned in the town, but they have an uphill battle ahead of them to really clean up the place.

Apart from the rubbish disposal problem, which elicited loud disgusted comments from Andy and mutterings from the rest of us, life was pretty pleasant at Snow Height. It was enlivened by the regular comings and goings of casual visitors who would stay a few nights. These people paid hotel rates for their accommodation, and were provided with bedding and even room service. The staff would cook up glasses of chai and simple meals on a hotplate in the little kitchen-cum-storeroom behind the shop.

The visitors were mostly Indians coming to the hills for a few days' break, or foreign Buddhists in town for the teachings. They generally stayed in one of the three rooms alongside mine. One of the few disadvantages of my location was that I was occasionally woken by someone having an animated cell phone conversation on the balcony outside my room.

Evening entertainment wasn't a big feature of life in Dharamshala, but some of the Russian Buddhists made up for this by organising their own. One night during the Dalai Lama's teachings I was woken by a loud rapping on my door at about 2.30am. I struggled out of bed to find a small and obviously tipsy young Russian woman. She giggled a bit and then scampered away to look for her friends by banging on someone else's door. Another night I was entertained by hours of chanting and bell ringing from the neighbouring room, where some of her more sober compatriots were conducting some sort of ritual.

There were also many animal visitors at Snow Height. Cows regularly strolled up the staircase and nosed around the washing hanging on the clothesline. The old goatherd's flock would sometimes venture up the stairs once they'd finished rootling through the rubbish bags. One morning I came out onto my balcony to talk to Andy, and a startled mongoose shot out of the drain at my feet and raced away to safety under a pile of wood.

Another day I found my balcony strewn with bits of chapatti, and a visiting Indian woman said she'd chased away a couple of monkeys who were sitting on the railing having a snack. She also told me that in Delhi where she lived she had quite a problem with monkeys coming into her kitchen, opening the fridge and stealing eggs.

All the teachers except me had had monkeys in their rooms. I only escaped because the others had learned to keep their doors shut, and passed the information on to me. However, one Sunday afternoon I was reading on my bed when I heard a roar of rage from Andy's room, and then a shriek from Suzette. A big monkey had come into Andy's room and beat a hasty retreat when he shouted at it. It then darted into Suzette's room next door. She was having a snooze and woke with a start.

"All I could think of to do," she said, "Was pull the blanket over my head and hope it went away." Fortunately it left, though not before grabbing a banana. We had not seen monkeys around the apartments for a while and Suzette and Andy had relaxed their vigilance.

I loved seeing the monkey families swinging through the forest and sauntering along the road. They seemed so at home in the environment, and were free to come and go as they pleased. However, at close quarters they could be alarming because they moved so fast and would hiss and bare their teeth if they felt threatened. I was very glad I never had one in my room.

I often used to drag one of my wooden lounge chairs onto the balcony, and sit enjoying the view and the action on the street. There were always people coming up and down the road, cars, motorbikes, cawing crows, the donkey brigade, Tibet Charity students who would wave as they went past, the goat man and his flock, a stray dog taking a walk, a meandering cow or two, or a kite swooping down over the trees in search of prey.

In an apartment building on the hill directly above Tibet Charity lived a German aging hippy who had adopted several stray dogs. Every afternoon she would bring them down the stairs beside Tibet Charity and take them for a walk. Every day without fail, the Tibet Charity dogs would see the interlopers passing by on 'their' stairs and go completely berserk. There would be a few minutes of shouting and frenzied barking and growling as the German got her charges safely down to the street. Then she would stride out into the road holding a massive staff, as Andy said, "Like Moses parting the waters," and force any passing traffic to screech to a halt while her dogs crossed the road. Then they would all shamble off to walk the kora. I was really glad I never met them while I was doing the circuit, as they were not at all conducive to a peaceful, meditative atmosphere.

Around November, the Snow Height staff were suddenly galvanised into action and spent several days clearing an area of scrubby land behind the washing line. After they'd levelled a small section, they started carrying planks of wood and sheets of corrugated iron onto the site. We speculated about

101

what they were doing, and decided they were building a storage hut for the various bits of wood and metal stacked around the area. Sure enough within a couple of days a rickety and very basic hut had appeared.

However, this was India and huts were far too precious for just storing bits and pieces. Within a week, an Indian family had moved in - mother, father and two very small children. The weather was getting quite chilly by this time and the hut seemed totally inadequate to our Western eyes, but they seemed to cope.

The only other time the Snow Height staff got really animated was during Diwali, the festival of light in early November.

The festival of Diwali celebrates the defeat of the demon king Ravana by Lord Rama. When Rama returned in triumph to his capital Ayodhya after a long absence, the people illuminated the city with oil lamps and firecrackers.

Indians celebrate Diwali by lighting small clay lamps filled with oil to signify the triumph of good over evil. People wear new clothes, and most Indian business communities begin the financial year on the first day of the festival.

As far as we were concerned, Diwali in McLo seemed mainly to feature lots and lots of fireworks. For about a week beforehand you could hear random bursts and bangs at all times of the day. Several times I was walking down the narrow streets of the town when a huge flash and bang would roar out just ahead, as if a bomb had gone off. The first few times it happened I nearly jumped out of my skin.

On the actual date of the Diwali festival, which also happened to be Guy Fawkes Day, Ron, Suzette and I walked up to town in the early evening to have dinner. All around we could see people carrying bags and boxes of fire crackers. Outside one particularly quiet hotel near the temple where few guests ever seemed to stay, the Indian staff were gleefully unloading an enormous box of fireworks.

We decided to eat at Kailash, an upstairs restaurant in the centre of town. By the time our food arrived it was dark and it felt as if war had broken out. Our meal was punctuated by thunderous bangs and flashes from outside on the street. Down in the valley around lower Dharamshala there were skyrockets shooting off in every direction. The festival of Diwali was evidently in full swing.

As we walked back through town, a fountain of rockets was erupting from the roof of the quiet hotel near the temple.

At Snow Height we found the normally restrained manager and his staff well underway with their own Diwali celebration. They had decorated the balconies of the apartments with little candles which looked beautiful glowing steadily in the still night.

The Snow Height staff had also gathered a fine stock of fireworks and were busily setting them off in the road, with lots of laughter and shouting and a total disdain for anything resembling health and safety. They were hurling firecrackers about, letting off rockets in all directions and bowling Catherine wheels down the road in a spectacular display that only puttered out when they fell into the open drain. It was a bit alarming but great fun to watch.

The next day the men were back to their usual quiet selves, but they had done their best to celebrate Diwali in style.

*Chapter Twenty-two*

# *"Nga Pö-yig lobjung ki yö."*

The Tibet Charity term was due to finish in early December. All the schools would be shut during the cold, snowy months of January and February. I got the impression that the town more or less closed down during this time. Ron was staying on until March, and said he really enjoyed the more peaceful atmosphere of the winter months.

We certainly noticed a gradual exodus of stallholders from the streets, starting in mid November. I heard that many of them went to other places in India such as Bodh Gaya, where there is a brisk trade in pilgrimages and Buddhist tourism.

One Sunday in late November, Andy and I walked up to Dharamkot for lunch. The usually busy Tipa Road was very quiet except for a few monkeys, and Dharamkot was almost deserted. The Israeli tourist season was obviously over and most of the hotels were closed.

We ate lunch in an Indian café strangely decorated with lurid murals of Indian gods and other figures. It looked as though the painter had been on some kind of illicit substance. There were a few rumours of drugs in Dharamshala, although I never came across any. The weirdest story I heard was that of a crazed Israeli man who was supposed to have run down the kora naked, slipped and fallen over the side of the path and broken his leg.

After lunch, Andy and I strolled through the fields past a large hotel in a state of semi decay. Apparently it was still open for business, as there was a group of young foreigners standing on a balcony. They included a man dressed in Orthodox Jewish clothing, complete with long side locks and black hat. We called up to them, "What's the hotel like?" and they said it was OK.

"Are you Jewish?" they asked us, and when we said we weren't, the Orthodox Jew shouted, "Do you want to be?"

As the end of term drew near we all concentrated on revision and encouraged our students to study hard for the end-of-year exam. I was pretty confident that if they revised their work thoroughly most of my class would pass and be eligible for the intermediate class, although I actually felt that Dawa, who was still struggling, would be better off if she repeated the pre-intermediate course.

I was also studying in my spare time for my Tibetan exam. There were only six of us who had been in the class for the full three months and were eligible to sit the exam. Ani-la had persuaded us to sit by telling us it would be "very easy." I was quite nervous about doing the test as we had never really done much reading aloud, and it apparently included an oral section. However, I told myself it didn't matter if I failed and it would be fun if I passed, so I tried to revise in a relaxed fashion.

The Tibet Charity students sat their exam and, in the evening, my class all went out for dinner at Kailash restaurant. It was a great night. Everyone was relieved to have the test behind them, and there was plenty of laughter, teasing and singing.

Unfortunately, that night I developed a nasty sore throat. Instead of studying Tibetan I spent most of the next few days in bed, feeling pretty ill. Eventually I dragged myself over to the Tibet Charity health clinic, where the nurse gave me some Ayurvedic pills to take and lozenges to suck.

During this low time I really appreciated Andy's concern. Several times he went up to town and brought me back a meal, and each morning he would bring down a pot of porridge for my breakfast. My lovely student Lhamo also heard I was ill and came over with a big thermos of lemon ginger honey tea which she refilled every day.

I don't know if it was because I wasn't feeling well, but I couldn't seem to remember much of the Tibetan I tried to learn, no matter how hard I tried. So on the day of the Tibetan exam I set off for the Library feeling very nervous. The sore throat had gone but I was left with a heavy cold and a graveyard cough, and my brain felt quite fuzzy.

*Well, the exam wasn't exactly a roaring success,* I wrote in my diary that afternoon. We first had to write out the Tibetan consonants and a set of sub-joined letters. This was straightforward enough and I managed to translate a few simple sentences into Tibetan, but giving the honorific forms of a list of words was completely beyond me.

Then came the reading component. I had already finished as much as I could manage of the written exam, so I volunteered to be the first to do the oral test. I was horrified to be handed a full A4 page of Tibetan words and told to sight read them. Tibetan pronunciation depends on identifying the root letter of a syllable and knowing how the sound may be influenced by the suffix and post-suffix (if any). It's definitely not something you want to attempt with a badly functioning brain.

I made my way slowly back up the hill to Snow Height, wondering sourly about Ani-la's assurance that the exam would be "easy," and speculating on what a "difficult" exam would have looked like. However, it was over, and I could concentrate on marking my own students' exams and writing out their certificates. All but Dawa had passed and even she had done better than I had expected.

The prize-giving ceremony took place on the terrace at Tibet Charity, under a beautiful canopy specially brought in for the occasion. The day was cool and still and the mountains stood out against the pale blue sky as we gathered for the last time.

The ceremony started off quite formally with speeches by the two top students from Suzette's upper-intermediate class. Jigmey - who had come from Tibet as a teenager and ended up having heart surgery - spoke confidently and fluently about coming to India with no English, and starting in the absolute beginners' class three years earlier. If anything was going to make us feel our volunteering was worthwhile, this story was. I think we all had lumps in our throats. Jigmey ended her speech to enthusiastic applause.

Then it was the teachers' turn to each make a short speech. I had not thought a lot about what I was going to say, and was more concerned about getting through it without coughing all over the microphone. Just before I got up to speak the Director hissed at me, "You will say something in Tibetan?"

*No pressure, then!* I thought, and managed to include "Nga Pö-yig lobjung ki yö." I hoped this meant, "I am learning Tibetan." The elderly monk who was the guest of honour looked a bit puzzled but the Director seemed pleased. I told the students I had loved teaching them and hoped to come back one day.

After the certificates were given out to the top students in each class - in my case to Suchin and Mingma - every class presented a short entertainment. We teachers had all been rather alarmed when we were told our classes would have to do a presentation, as we were given barely any notice of this before the exams, and had very little time to practise.

Each of us dealt with the challenge in a different way. Andy and Suzette's classes both did Christmas songs. Lindy's students recited a poem. I had found a copy of the Dalai Lama's advice *Never Give Up* and my students took turns to recite this. It seemed to go down very well with the elderly monk. Lhamo rounded off our presentation with a song from Amdo, her home region of Tibet.

Relieved to get this ordeal over, we were able to relax and enjoy Norbu's beginner monks doing their Bob Marley song. Then the floor was opened up to anyone who wanted to have a go. The student nurses had been waiting for this moment and took to the stage, dressed in their best chubas. While they were presenting a couple of traditional songs and dances, Suzette suggested in a whisper that we teachers should "do something." She had a CD of Christmas songs with her and thought we could sing along to *Rudolf the Red-Nosed Reindeer.*

Tibetans love to laugh at others making fools of themselves so we could hardly fail to be a hit, even if we completely muffed our performance. I was still plagued by the cough so I couldn't really sing. As the music started I hit on the idea of doing actions. It was a riot! The students roared! The other teachers played along and we brought the house down.

Lunch was a welcome break. Dekyi and Mr Moon had produced a delicious spread, more ambitious than the usual dahl, rice and veg. Dessert was provided by Andy who had thoughtfully bought enough ice cream for the entire school.

The afternoon was party time. There were more songs and a traditional round dance. Most people joined in (though not the monks) and the teachers were soon draped with layers of khatas by our students. I received Christmas cards (Santa Claus with a *Free Tibet* sign) and gifts from Dawa and Lhamo, who gave me a particularly long khata "For long life."

The student nurses were well into their stride when we left, and the event was rapidly turning into a riotous karaoke session.

*What a fun day that turned out to be!* I wrote in my diary that night.

# Chapter Twenty-three

# *By taxi to the Punjab*

The foreign teachers were due to leave Dharamshala at the end of term. We had all been thinking about what we were going to do during the final part of our time in India.

Lindy and Suzette were well organised. They had been to a local travel agent and booked a hectic two week tour to Delhi, Agra, Varanasi and Bodh Gaya. Then Suzette was going to fly back to California while Lindy went to visit a friend in France.

Andy kept saying he couldn't wait to leave India, and had booked the first available night bus to Delhi after the end of term. He was planning a holiday in Thailand and a quick trip to the USA before starting his next teaching contract in Japan.

I was torn between conflicting emotions. On the one hand I was excited about seeing the family in New Zealand, and there was Christmas to look forward to. On the other hand I was really sad at the thought of leaving Dharamshala. I'd settled into a very pleasant routine, every day was interesting, I was starting to make some headway into understanding Buddhism and I'd come to feel very much at home in McLo.

I had several days to spare between the end of term and the date of my flight from Delhi, but I felt very ambivalent about being a tourist in India. I had come to Dharamshala with the idea of staying somewhere and getting to know it well, and I really didn't want to just take a superficial glance at other parts of India. On the other hand, I might never come back. Maybe I should visit places like Amritsar and Agra while I had the chance?

I consulted Suzette and Lindy's travel agent, Kamal, and asked him to suggest an itinerary which would get me to Delhi in time to catch my flight on the evening of 21 December. He came up with a tour to Amritsar, the bizarre military ceremonial at Wagah on the India/Pakistan border, and the Taj Mahal in Agra. It looked interesting, but the tour involved a lot of travelling and was pretty expensive.

In a WiFi café that afternoon, I went into Google Earth and checked out the geography between Dharamshala and Delhi. I noticed the city of Chandigarh almost half way between the two. According to Wikipedia, Chandigarh was the first planned city in India, designed by the famous French architect Le Corbusier as the new capital of the Indian Punjab after partition.

Three facts about Chandigarh leapt out at me. Firstly, the city had one of India's most visited tourist attractions, a strange Rock Garden created by an eccentric genius called Nek Chand. Secondly, it was reputed to be the richest city in India. And, best of all, Le Corbusier had designed the city on a grid pattern divided into square Sectors with wide, well signposted streets and lots of trees.

So, I would have somewhere interesting to visit, the city was not a distressing sinkhole of grinding poverty, it sounded attractive and it was easy to get around. To someone who regularly gets lost in strange places this was a definite plus.

I went back to Kamal and asked him to send me to Chandigarh and from there to Delhi.

"Why do you want to go to Chandigarh? There's nothing there!"

I mentioned the famous Rock Garden and Le Corbusier. He clearly thought I was crazy, but a customer was a customer, and he would help me get there if that was what I wanted. However, there were no direct buses - I would have to take a taxi as far as Chandigarh. I could then go by train to Delhi. I happily agreed.

The last few days in McLo sped by. I was surprised to find I'd passed the Tibetan exam and attended the certificate ceremony on the roof of the Library. It was much more conventional and less fun than the Tibet Charity prize giving.

I bought a few last minute gifts and sorted out various things I didn't want to take home, to make space for my purchases in my bag. Between us, Lindy, Suzette and I had quite a lot of clothing and other items to give away, so we piled it all into a taxi and took it to the Tibetan Children's Village where it was gratefully received.

On our last day together, the foreign teachers, Norbu and Ron all had a last round of beers together on the roof of the Ashoka restaurant. It was a lovely crisp day and the mountains with a dusting of snow stood out against the blue sky. The black-shouldered kites were wheeling and swooping above us. I loved watching these magnificent birds of prey but I'd never been close enough to photograph them before. Now at last I got a fine photo of a kite as it passed low overhead.

As I walked back to Snow Height, I met my star student Mingma who was also preparing to leave town. He and his grandfather were going on a pilgrimage to Bodh Gaya, where the Buddha attained Enlightenment under the Bodhi tree. While we were celebrating Christmas in New Zealand, Mingma and his family would be performing thousands of prostrations in one of Buddhism's most sacred places.

Andy, Lindy and Suzette all left McLo the following day. Andy went by bus to Delhi and the women took a taxi to the railway station at Pathankot on the first leg of their tour.

Far too soon, it was my own last morning in McLo. I had breakfast and then walked the kora for the final time, carrying a bundle containing my sheets, a yak wool rug and my plastic bowl and spoon. I planned to give them to a beggar family living in an open shelter not far from the Dalai Lama's temple. I spun the prayer wheels, murmured my mantra "May Tibet be free in the Dalai Lama's *current* lifetime," and climbed the hill to the beggars' shelter. To my surprise it was empty. The family had gone. However, in Dharamshala a beggar is never very far away so I gave my bundle to the next one I met - a cheery man with a heavily bandaged foot -  and went on my way.

The taxi, a Toyota people mover, arrived on time at 10 o'clock. The driver slung my bags into the boot, I said goodbye to Ron to whom I bequeathed my hot water bottle (originally Naomi's), hugged Lhamo who had come with yet another khata to see me off, and climbed aboard.

It felt a bit odd to be the only passenger in such a big taxi, but as we made our way through lower Dharamshala and out into the countryside I began to appreciate it, as the roads became progressively worse and more potholed.

My driver was an Indian man past middle age, rather taciturn but friendly enough. He seemed to be a careful driver. This was a definite bonus as some taxi drivers were frighteningly gung ho at overtaking. I assured him I was in no hurry to get to Chandigarh and we went along at a reasonable speed. This was just as well for the health of the local monkeys, who seemed to delight in sitting in the middle of the road.

We had been going for about an hour when the driver asked if I wanted chai, and we stopped in the next village. By a strange coincidence, this happened to be where he lived. It was in the tea growing region of Kangra, a quiet little farming area where life seemed to be going on at a leisurely pace.

We drove further down toward the plains and the road became increasingly marginal and more dusty. Everything in the villages we passed was covered in a thick layer of dust.

Later, I noted in my diary what I'd seen that morning: a blacksmith shoeing a horse by the side of the road; a barber shaving a customer under a tree; a heavily laden motorbike whose load had included a child's tricycle; hand-operated communal water pumps in the villages; terraced rice paddies and several herds of long-eared sheep and goats. The villages mostly comprised rows of very rickety shops made of corrugated iron, with the occasional incongruous sign for a Cyber café.

I was starting to get really hungry by the time we drove into the town of Una, turned down a narrow alleyway and parked in front of the Hotel Maya Deluxe. The receptionist directed me to a gloomy restaurant with heavy wooden furniture and the air conditioning turned on far too high - it was like sitting in a fridge. However, the malai kofta I ordered was delicious, and I was entertained by the comings and goings of people in the bus station outside.

As we drove out of town, I was interested to spot a couple of Tibetan street sellers with their goods spread out on a blanket. They were the first Tibetans I had seen since we left Dharamshala.

For about half an hour the road continued to be so bad I could hardly believe we were on a main route. Then, a miracle happened. Suddenly we were driving along a tar-sealed two-lane road which soon became a four-lane highway. The driver explained that we had crossed the line from the poor state of Himachal Pradesh to the wealthy Punjab.

The difference in the landscape was dramatic. There was a wide canal running along beside the road. The farms looked larger and the buildings less decrepit. There was still a lot to see - a flock of white egrets in a field, a sinister gathering of vultures on a rubbish dump, a man at a roadside stall squeezing sugar cane juice, and many people lounging on charpoys in the shade outside their houses. I noticed more men in turbans and many Sikh temples along the road.

The road became much more congested as we neared Chandigarh. We crawled along, weaving our way around a mass of buses, cars, tuk tuks, donkey carts and bicycles. However, we made steady progress and before long were bowling along the wide boulevards of the city, looking for my hotel in Sector 22. We found it without too much trouble, jammed between a motor repair shop and a dingy little restaurant - the Kailash Palace Hotel.

Kamal the travel agent had never sent anyone to Chandigarh before, so he couldn't recommend a hotel. I had trawled the internet and found the Kailash Palace. I was attracted by the name *Kailash* (Tibet's most sacred mountain), it was in my price range and the reviews were lukewarm rather than negative. An inner voice told me any hotel with the name

*Palace* at that price was bound to be a dump, but I booked it anyway.

There was good news and bad news about the Hotel Kailash Palace. The receptionist was a jolly middle-aged Indian who was extremely helpful and positive. I liked him immediately, even though we had a brief run-in because I didn't have a printed receipt for my booking.

When I got to my room, I found it had no windows. This was bad news because five minutes after I moved in there was a power cut. Luckily I had become used to frequent power failures in Dharamshala and kept my torch handy. Well, it was a bit gloomy and there was no hot water, but it was in the middle of town and I was only there for two nights. I unpacked what I needed and set off to explore.

Each Sector in Chandigarh is basically a very large city block. Sector 22 had shops around the outside and a pleasant looking residential area in the centre of the block. I felt like a country bumpkin as I walked down the wide pavement. A pavement! I hadn't seen one for three months! Between the pavement and the road itself was a spacious parking area, so for the first time in ages I didn't have to worry about cars coming up behind me and tooting in my ear. It felt quite luxurious.

Most of the shops were a lot more up-market than in McLeod Ganj. There were several fashionable and expensive dress shops, some classy restaurants, a store with huge TVs in the window and a deli with French camembert and Italian olive oils. Alongside these shops were the more ordinary places, such as the grimy internet café where I printed off my booking receipt for the friendly Kailash Palace receptionist.

I wasn't hungry enough to warrant a meal in one of the posh restaurants, so I decided to eat in the ordinary-looking little Family Restaurant beside the Palace. I ordered chow mein, thinking it would be a light tasty meal, but when I took my first mouthful I nearly spat it all over the table. I don't know how many chillies it contained, but it was so fiery I found it impossible to eat. The waiter and I seemed to have no common language, so in the end I just paid for the nearly untouched meal, bought a packet of biscuits and left.

Luckily, I had brought my handy little kettle from Dharamshala, so I could brew up a cup of tea. Without any windows the room was a bit stuffy, but the fan moved the air around and I slept well.

*Chapter Twenty-four*

# *An eccentric wonderland*

Early the next morning I took a bicycle rickshaw to Chandigarh's most visited attraction, the Nek Chand Rock Garden. The wide, flat roads were lined with trees and the traffic flowed freely so it was a really pleasant drive, apart from the constant whining of my driver. He would have much preferred to take me to the Rose Garden instead of the Rock Garden because it was a shorter distance to pedal.

Wikipedia has this to say about Nek Chand and his Rock Garden:

*Nek Chand was a roading inspector who began collecting materials from demolition sites around the city in the 1950s. He recycled these materials into his own vision of the divine kingdom of Sukrani, choosing a gorge in a forest near Sukhna Lake in Chandigarh for his work. The gorge had been designated as a land conservancy, a forest buffer established in 1902 that nothing could be built on.*

*Chand's work was illegal, but he was able to hide it for eighteen years before it was discovered by the authorities in 1975. By this time, it had grown into a 12-acre complex of interlinked courtyards, each filled with hundreds of pottery-covered concrete sculptures of dancers, musicians, and animals.*

*His work was in serious danger of being demolished, but he was able to get public opinion on his side, and in 1976 the park was inaugurated as a public space. Nek Chand was given a salary, a title ('Sub-Divisional Engineer, Rock Garden') and a workforce of fifty labourers so he could concentrate full-time on his work. It even appeared on an Indian stamp in 1983. The*

*Rock Garden is still made out of recycled materials; and with the government's help, Chand was able to set up collection centres around the city for waste, especially rags and broken ceramics.*

At the Rock Garden, a crudely painted sign outside the kiosk read:
*Admission: Adult 10 years to 100 years, 10 rupees. Above 100, free!*

That evening I wrote in my diary: *It was like a mixture of a funfair and Gaudi's Parc Güell in Barcelona.*

The various areas of the garden were divided by high, meandering walls with low gateways and tunnels built of mosaic-covered concrete. Most of the mosaics were made of broken crockery but I also saw chunks of ceramic isolators from power lines, broken glass and unidentifiable bits of pottery.

Once Nek Chand had got an idea into his head, he liked to work it to death. One area was filled with crowds of grinning identical toothy animals which vaguely resembled reindeer. In another, there were at least a hundred female figures arranged in straight rows. They were about a metre high, with multi-coloured saris, and stared straight ahead through white ceramic eyes. Built on the same basic plan, the position of the arms - lifted, by the sides, gesticulating and so on - gave the crowd a touch of variety, but also added to the slight sense of eeriness about the display.

I felt a little as if I had landed on another planet. I wandered on through seemingly endless different areas, past groups of musicians, seated figures, standing figures, gods, monkeys, dancers, birds, figures with three heads, and other bizarre and unidentifiable creatures.

Reality and artifice were occasionally hard to separate. In one section there was a large baobab tree with a mass of twisted roots cascading down a wall, and I only realised as I looked more closely that concrete roots had been intertwined with the tree's own root system. A dirty little stream ran along beside the path by the tree. Looking up, I saw a miniature village with houses and temples perched on the top of the high bank above me.

I found I was not only an observer, but an object of intense scrutiny as well. Long lines of school children were looping around the garden, and many of them seemed to find me at least as interesting as the art works. There were lots of giggles and waves and the occasional "Hello, how are you?" as we passed each other.

Eventually I emerged from yet another crockery-encrusted tunnel into a big open space. This was obviously the centre of the garden. It was here that the funfair aspect of the place was most apparent.

At one end was a massive concrete arcade of about twenty arches topped with huge white horses. Underneath each arch, long chains supported a big wooden swing. Both children and adults were happily playing on the swings.

As I made my way around the space, I found a hall of mirrors, a little refreshment kiosk and an aquarium. A lively crowd was dancing to loud music on a raised concrete dance floor, the men and women in separate groups.

The mosiacs on the surrounding walls in this area were the most sophisticated and colourful I had seen so far, with some really lovely representations of animals, peacocks, monkeys and various abstract patterns.

On one side was a kind of arena with tiers of wide steps covered in bright mosaics. Just in front of the steps was a full-sized stuffed camel with an elaborate saddle and bridle. If you paid the turbaned men in charge, you could climb on board and pose for pictures. The camel was even jointed so it swayed slightly in a lifelike way.

But just a minute! I distinctly saw the camel blink as I walked past. It was alive all right, and stood staring around with a disdainful expression on its face. Not much of a way to spend one's life, and I think I would have preferred a stuffed one after all.

I bought a bottle of mango drink and sat on a mosaic-covered wall under a tree, watching the animated crowd. How wise the locals had been to protect this unique expression of eccentric art, and now here they were, swinging, dancing, chatting and generally having fun.

I was approached by two high school boys with a microphone.

"Excuse me, madam. We are from Mt Carmel School. Can I ask you what you think of the Nek Chand Rock Garden?"

"It's one of the most amazing things I've ever seen," I said, which was true.

"And what do you think about the city of Chandigarh?"

"I like it," I replied. "It seems like a prosperous city, it's easy to get around, and you have lovely wide streets and plenty of trees. I'm enjoying my visit very much."

They were obviously intensely proud of their city and were on a *Clean up Chandigarh* campaign, encouraging people to pick up their waste. I wished them luck with it. Although the level of garbage was not on a par with Dharmashala, there was still a fair amount of rubbish strewn around the city.

It was now early afternoon. I had read that Chandigarh had a number of good museums. They all seemed to be clustered around the same part of town, so I decided to have a look. I eventually made my way back to the entrance after following a few false trails. Once I got there it was very easy to book a bicycle rickshaw at a pre-pay booth outside the gate, and within a few minutes we were on our way to the Museum sector.

The driver dropped me outside the art museum, a blocky affair designed by Le Corbusier and located in a spacious park. Inside I paid my 10-rupee entry fee plus a 5-rupee charge for using a camera.

The museum had plenty of bored-looking guards, but I seemed to be virtually the only visitor, and I had a marvellous time. I began with a lovely display of textiles, including a couple of very old Tibetan thangkas and some exquisite

119

examples of Kantha embroidery. All the labels on the exhibits were conveniently written in English.

As I climbed the stairs to the upper level, I paused to admire some reproductions of Buddhist frescoes from the Ajanta caves in Maharashtra.

Upstairs, I came across a beautiful collection of small bronze statues of graceful Indian gods and goddesses, musicians and dancers. In another room, a large exhibition traced the way in which the image of the Buddha has changed through the centuries.

From there I wandered into a room full of modern art. This interested me less than the next area, where there was a display of Indian miniature paintings from the Mughal era. They were like little jewels; exquisitely detailed paintings of Rajas and their courtiers, dancers, musicians, elephants and camels, as well as a few works depicting the daily life of ordinary Indians. One of my favourites was a lively drawing of a man being chased by a dog, losing his shoe and upsetting a pot in his panic.

By this time it was mid afternoon. I had only had a bottle of juice since breakfast so I was starting to feel really hungry. Outside the museum gates, I hailed a passing rickshaw and headed back to Sector 22. Earlier I had noticed a sign saying *Nik's Bakers*. It seemed like a good place for a meal.

Nik's Bakers features in *Lonely Planet* as number seven in '70 things to do in Chandigarh.' (The Nek Chand Garden is second behind a fancy Chinese restaurant.) It could best be described as a multiethnic fast food joint. The illustrated menu featured Indian, Chinese and Italian food, toasted sandwiches, ice cream, cakes and lots of lurid looking desserts. I ordered green tea and a grilled cheese and mushroom sandwich. It arrived at my table within a few minutes. The sandwich was stuffed full of mushrooms and came with a side order of very good French fries.

I paid 173 rupees including a tip for the waiter. This made it the most expensive meal I had eaten so far in India but it was delicious and very filling. Price didn't seem to be a problem for the locals - the place was very noisy and full of families and couples, many of whom had chosen the Western foods on the menu.

I left Nik's feeling full and satisfied and walked the five minutes round the block to my hotel, blessing Le Corbusier and his grid-based town planning.

# Chapter Twenty-five

# Street kids and the Salaam Baalak Trust

The next morning I was booked on an early train to Delhi so I got up just before six o'clock, had tea and biscuits, and humped my bags down to the reception desk. The desk clerk and his assistant were bundled up in blankets on the floor, but they woke up and the assistant came downstairs and hailed a passing tuk tuk. The grumpy driver wasn't at all keen to drive the eight kilometres to the station in the chill pre-dawn air. Eventually we agreed on a slightly higher price and off we went. I was very glad of my Kashmir silk/wool shawl as it really was quite cold.

At the station, a helpful passer-by directed me to the right platform but said, "The train is an hour late." I found a free corner by the station master's office and settled down to wait. The station was crowded with people, many of them wrapped in blankets and shawls. Several trains came and went. After nearly an hour, by which time I was really looking forward to the arrival of the Delhi train, there came an announcement over the loudspeaker to say it was further delayed by half an hour.

The train finally rumbled into the station at about 9am. The 'chair car' was much more basic than I had expected. Fortunately, I had nobody sitting beside me so I could spread out a bit. There was a continuous stream of young men and boys through the carriage selling food and drink, but I decided visiting the toilet would be too problematic, and confined myself to sipping water and nibbling a few biscuits. This was one of the few times when I missed travelling with a companion, if only to have someone to help guard the luggage.

The train took around four hours to reach Delhi, rolling

through the dusty countryside past groups of people working in the fields, and occasional towns and villages. There would often be a group of men and boys playing cricket outside the village, while the women sat around in companionable groups. As we neared Delhi we passed through some very fetid-looking slums with rudimentary dwellings perched beside horrible rubbish-filled pools of water.

The train pulled into New Delhi railway station and everyone struggled off the train. By now I was feeling tired, hungry and irritable and my pack seemed ridiculously heavy. The station was jammed with people and I had no idea where the exit was. A man approached me.

"Taxi, madam? Do you have a hotel?"

"Yes, the Ajanta."

"Your booking at the Ajanta is not confirmed. I must take you to the booking office."

Luckily, I had heard of this scam for extorting money out of unwary tourists and snarled, "Either you take me to the Ajanta hotel or no taxi!" He rapidly disappeared.

I was starting to feel more frazzled by the moment and my bag was killing me. Luckily I could see the exit by this time and pushed my way toward it. Outside, two more young men approached me offering a taxi. This time they seemed to be genuine, so we fixed a price and made our way to their battered taxi in the carpark.

The Ajanta Hotel was only a short ride away. A smart doorman took my bags inside, check-in was straightforward and included a cup of chai, a porter carried my pack to my room and I was finally able to relax. So far it had been a very long day.

Kamal the travel agent had booked the Ajanta for me. It turned out to be a good mid-range Delhi hotel, clean and comfortable without being too expensive. The shower was hot, there were tea-making facilities in my room, the TV worked and the food in the restaurant was good. It was certainly a welcome step up from the Kailash Palace.

The next morning, after a very good buffet breakfast, I walked back down the road toward New Delhi railway station, this time thankfully without my heavy pack.

One day when Lindy, Suzette and I were in Bhagsu we had seen a poster advertising walking tours in Delhi, presented by the Salaam Baalak Trust. It certainly didn't sound like your average tourist experience:

*Nobody knows Delhi's streets better than the young people who will be your guides. The streets were their only home until Salaam Baalak Trust offered them a chance for a new life.*

I reached the meeting point for the walking tour near the New Delhi station gates, to find several other people waiting. They included an English couple, two American men and a family of Indian women and girls. Our guide Satender introduced himself and said it was the first time he had taken Indians on the tour. "I'm quite nervous," he said.

He certainly didn't look it, and I was impressed by his assurance as he launched into his spiel. He told us he was eighteen and had arrived in Delhi at the age of thirteen. His father had beaten him regularly when he was a child, and he had finally decided to run away and try his luck elsewhere.

Satender told us something about how children end up on the streets of this chaotic city. Some have run away from bad experiences at home, but others have seen too many movies and have dreams of becoming Bollywood stars. Some children simply get lost in the crowd while on journeys or pilgrimages with their families. Having experienced the mass of people in the railway station the day before, I found this very easy to understand.

It really meant something when Satender told us about the lives of street children in Delhi, because we knew he had been one himself. The children sleep rough, often under railway bridges. They are easy targets for anyone who wants to exploit them - stall-holders who promise them work and don't feed or pay them, bullies, pimps and gangs. They live by their wits, collecting plastic bottles and old clothes for recycling, cleaning shoes, stealing, picking pockets and begging. Food is not their major problem as the nearby Sikh temple provides free food every day for thousands of people in Delhi. Any money the children earn tends to be frittered away on video games, drugs, alcohol and glue. The kids may spend months on the streets before being picked up by the police or people who know about the work of the Salaam Baalak Trust.

The Trust aims to either return rescued children to their homes, or give them full residential care and an education. When Satender was rescued, he initially refused to tell the Trust social worker where he came from, because he was afraid that he would be sent home. When eventually he did gain enough confidence to give them the information, he was given a choice - go back to his father, who was still violent, or stay with the Trust. He had obviously made the right choice. He had recently graduated from high school, had a good job with the Trust and had his eye on further education in IT - an interest he said he'd picked up while playing video games as a street kid.

The tour took us through a maze of narrow streets and alleyways. I would have been nervous about venturing down them on my own, if only through fear of getting lost. Satender pointed out areas of interest, such as the place where the kids sold the plastic bottles they collected, right next to a grubby shack full of video games. We also visited a day centre above Delhi railway station where street children can come to have a rest, get some education and see a volunteer doctor. Like Satender, many street kids take time to gain confidence in the Trust so the day centre acts as a half-way house.

To end the tour, Satender and his helper Ajay led us to one of the Trust's six shelter homes in Delhi. We climbed two flights of stairs and entered a room decorated with cheerful murals and piled with mattresses. The room next door was full of lively-looking boys having a lesson. Looking around, I was struck by the humour and intelligence on their faces. These kids were survivors, and with the Trust behind them they obviously had a good chance of a future.

These were some of the roughly one thousand children - boys and girls - who are being cared for by the Trust. It has a staff of around a hundred and twenty, but also welcomes volunteer help. The surroundings were basic, but the place radiated confidence and optimism.

Photos and short statements by some of the older ex-street kids were pinned on the wall. They wanted to be IT specialists, musicians, chess players and engineers. Satender told us one of India's most celebrated photographers is a former Salaam Baalak boy.

Looking at the faces of my fellow tourists as we ended the tour and thanked our guides, I could tell they were as moved and impressed as I was by the experience.

# Chapter Twenty-six

# *"Madam, I will help you."*

I decided not to try and do too much in Delhi, as I only had a short time before catching my plane. I really wanted to visit the National Museum, so the next morning I caught a tuk tuk and was carried for several kilometres through the hectic traffic and the exhaust fumes. It was early morning and many of the tuk tuks and horse drawn taxis were packed with children in their neat uniforms on their way to school. I also saw a record number of people on one motorbike - a man and four children.

Having paid my entry fee and entered the first exhibition gallery, my initial impression was that the collection could do with a jolly good dusting. The signage was dog-eared and grubby and the exhibits were arranged in an old fashioned, unimaginative way.

I soon discovered that the museum actually contained some real gems. One room had a fine display of artifacts from the early civilisations of the Indus valley. I was thrilled to recognise an exquisite little bronze statuette of a dancing girl from Mohenjodaro. I'd studied her in anthropology at university. Made around 2500 BC, she stands only nine centimetres high but poses with her hand on her hip, radiating confidence and personality.

Nearby, I found some other bronze wonders from the Indus Valley including a strange beast on wheels, about the size of a child's push-along toy. It resembled a cross between an elephant and a hippo. It seemed to be in perfect condition and I did a quick drawing of it, since I had opted not to pay the 300 rupee camera fee.

Next to it was an even more beautiful bronze piece, a lively model of a two-wheeled chariot drawn by two oxen. It was almost modernist in its simplicity. Picasso would have loved it. While I was sketching this wonderful piece of work, my concentration was challenged by a line of school children snaking their way through the room and past where I was drawing. There seemed to be at least a hundred students in each group. They were passing through the galleries at a terrific rate, urged on by the museum guards, so that it seemed impossible for them to see the exhibits properly. Most of them peered at what I was drawing as they whipped past, and a couple said, "That's very good!"

"No, *that's* very good," I said, pointing to the original. "Look at it, it's a masterpiece." They agreed politely and hurried on their way.

As in Chandigarh Museum, there was a very good collection of Buddha figures, including a reliquary containing some of the cremated relics of the Buddha himself. On the wall was a notice asking visitors not to make offerings before it. I also lingered for a long time in the room containing Hindu bronze figures, beautifully graceful and exquisitely detailed.

The Mughal painting section was the highlight of the museum. The exhibition space had been recently refurbished and a lot of care had been put into the display. There was a large exhibition containing some absolutely wonderful pieces, full of colour, life and detail.

I had a very tasty lunch in the museum cafeteria and then took a quick look around the textile section before deciding that museum fatigue was setting in. When I emerged from the building I noticed a very cute grey squirrel sitting perkily on top of the head of a stone bull, and was able to grab a quick photo before it darted off.

Back at the hotel I had a rest and then got ready to go to the airport. Kamal the travel agent had pre-paid my room and assured me that the hotel would run me to the airport for no charge. I suspected this might not be true, and was quite prepared to pay for transport to the airport if necessary.

When I approached the desk to check out, I got a shock when the clerk told me I still owed a night's rent. I had stayed two nights and most of a day, and had paid Kamal for three nights. However - and the clerk showed me the evidence in his ledger - Kamal had only paid the Ajanta for two nights.

With a sinking feeling I realised I had no receipt from Kamal, and was on very shaky ground if I wanted to avoid paying more money. We were talking about 2000 rupees. It wasn't an outrageously large sum, but there had been no room service during my stay and I had paid quite a lot for my meals and internet access, so I really felt they had done quite well out of me.

Thinking my best form of defence was attack, I started talking loudly about how I had intended to come back to the Ajanta, but would avoid it like the plague in future and, what's more, I would tell my many friends not to come to the hotel. I could see that I was starting to attract covert glances from other people in the lobby.

By this time I had pretty well exhausted my arguments and was about to make the best of a bad job and pay up, when the clerk looked at me solemnly and said, "Madam, I will help you because you are old. You do not have to pay."

*OK,* I thought, *Fine! For 2000 rupees I'm happy to be old!* We quite amicably sorted out the cost of a taxi - it turned out I did have to pay to go to the airport. The doorman summoned a cab, we all exchanged goodbyes in a most friendly fashion and I went on my way.

While we sat in the gridlocked rush hour traffic, I thought about the whole business of age in India. I was quite often asked my age in Dharamshala. Like the Indian tourists wanting to take our photos, it soon became another of those oddities about India that you learned to accept with good grace. What's more, whenever I said I was fifty-eight, the questioner would usually say reassuringly, "You look much younger!" Well, this time apparently I was old. So be it.

Actually I didn't feel old at all. Thanks to McLo's altitude and the constant walking up and down hills, I was fitter than I had been for years. My thighs hadn't been this firm since I was twenty! I had eaten a healthy, mostly vegetarian diet for three months. I had been living in a place where every day I was amazed and delighted by the people I met and the things I saw. I'd been constantly exposed to new ideas and interesting experiences, and I couldn't wait for whatever new adventures the future would bring.

Old? Hell no!

# Glossary of foreign words and abbreviations

**Amdo, Kham, U Tsang** Three areas of Tibet. U Tsang is the area around Lhasa and toward the west; Amdo is in the north east and Kham is in the south east.

**Ani-la** (Tibetan) Ani is a prefix added to the name of a nun in Tibetan Buddhism, roughly equivalent to "Sister." Ani also means aunt. The suffix -la (e.g. Ani-la) is a polite form used when talking to or about someone.

**Ayurvedic medicine** (Sanskrit, from Ayuveda - the complete knowledge for long life.) Ayurvedic medicine is a system of traditional medicine native to India, and a form of alternative medicine.

**Bodhisattva** (Sanskrit) An enlightened being; someone who, motivated by great compassion, has generated bodhicitta, a spontaneous wish to attain Buddhahood for the benefit of all sentient beings.

**CELTA** Certificate in English Language Teaching to Adults.

**Chai, masala chai** (Hindi) Indian spiced tea.

**Chapatti** (Hindi) Unleavened flat bread, also known as roti.

**Charpoy** (Hindi) A day bed used especially in India, consisting of a frame strung with tapes or light rope.

**Chuba** (Tibetan) Traditional costume of Tibet. The men's chuba is a long sleeved knee length coat with a tie belt, often worn with one arm slipped out of the sleeve. The women's long sleeved chuba is floor length, with a tie belt, also worn with one arm free. The everyday chuba for Tibetan women in Dharmashala is a floor length wrap-around sleeveless pinafore, worn over a brocade blouse. Married women also wear a multi-striped apron.

**Dependent origination** One of the most fundamental Buddhist teachings says that everything is interrelated. Nothing exists *independently* of other beings or phenomena. See **Emptiness.**

**Dharma** (Sanskrit) The Buddha's teachings; the way the teachings can be applied through ethical behaviour and the cultivation of mindfulness and wisdom.

**Dharamshala** (Hindi) A pilgrim refuge, sanctuary; from dharma and shala (Hindi); spiritual dwelling.

**Dhoti** (Hindi) Men's garment made from a rectangular piece of cloth seven yards long, wrapped around the waist and legs and knotted at the waist.

**Emptiness** In Buddhism, emptiness is related to **Dependent Origination**. Since everything is interrelated, then all beings and phenomena are 'empty' of *inherent* existence. This leads to one of the cornerstones of Tibetan Buddhism - the development of genuine compassion for all other sentient beings beside ourselves, since we are all equal in our desire for happiness and freedom from suffering.

**ESOL** English as a second language.

**Geshe** (Tibetan) Monastic scholar. The word Geshe is an abbreviation of a Tibetan expression meaning 'spiritual benefactor' or 'virtuous friend'. Gaining the Geshe qualification can take between twelve and twenty years of study, and is centred around textual memorisation and ritual debate.

**Karma** (Sanskrit) According to Buddhist theory, every time a person acts there is some quality of intention at the base of the mind. It is that quality rather than the outward appearance of the action which determines the effect. Karma is the factor which determines the realm of one's consequent rebirth in the cycle of **samsara** (the continuous flow of birth, life, death and rebirth). The karmic consequences of one's deeds and intentions may also be experienced in one's current life.

**Kantha** (Hindi) Embroidery from Bengal. Women use recycled material from saris and dhotis to create new layered textiles. These are decorated with fine colourful embroidery using a simple running or darning stitch. Muslim women create abstract patterns while Hindu women prefer to make scenes of daily life.

**Khata** (Tibetan) Traditional Tibetan ceremonial white silk scarf symbolising purity and compassion. It is given as a token of respect when ceremonially greeting or saying farewell to someone. A long khata symbolises the wish for the recipient to have a long life.

**Kora** (Tibetan) The ritual circuit around the Dalai Lama's temple in McLeod Ganj. It is customary to walk around the kora and other sacred sites such as temples and stupas in a clockwise direction.

**Lama** (Tibetan) Senior monk; scholar and teacher.

**Lingkhor** (Tibetan) The ritual circuit around the Dalai Lama's Potala Palace in Lhasa. It is replicated in McLeod Ganj by the kora.

**Majnu ka Tilla** (Hindi) Old area of Delhi, now the Tibetan enclave. Around a thousand Tibetans live here, in an area of less than a square kilometre.

**Mala** (Tibetan) Prayer beads, rosary.

**Malai kofta** (Hindi) Rich creamy tomato gravy with dumplings made of potato and paneer (cottage cheese).

**Mandala** Originally Sanskrit meaning "circle." An intricate design built on a square within a circle, representing a sacred space, a "Pure Buddha Realm"; an abode of fully realised beings or deities. Mandalas are used as aids to meditation and visualisation.

**Mani stone** (Tibetan) A stone carved and/or painted with *Om Mani Padme Hum*, the six syllabled mantra of Avalokiteshwara (Chenresig), the Bodhisattva of Compassion. Making or commissioning a mani stone is an act of devotion. Mani stones are placed in significant locations. In McLeod Ganj there are many mani stones along the **kora**.

**Mantra** (Sanskrit) A sound, syllable, word or group of words that can be used for deepening ones thought or, in the Buddhist context, for developing an enlightened mind.

**Metok** (Tibetan) Flower.

**Momo** (Tibetan) Tibetan dumpling made with vegetables, cheese, potato or mutton (originally yak meat).

**Mughal painting** Art created during the era of the Mughal Empire in India from the 16th to the 19th century. It follows a tradition of Persian miniature painting. Subjects include portraits, events and scenes from court life, animals and birds, hunting scenes, and illustrations of battles.

**Namaste** (Devanagari) Common Indian greeting meaning "Good Day" or "Greetings," with the implication "To be well." It is used when you meet or farewell someone.

**Nirvana** (Sanskrit) Enlightenment. The perfect peace of the state of mind that is free from craving, anger, and other afflicting states; being fully awake to the true nature of reality.

**Panchen Lama** (Tibetan) The highest ranking Lama after the Dalai Lama in the Gelug sect of Tibetan Buddhism. The present 11th incarnation of the Panchen Lama is a matter of controversy: the People's Republic of China asserts it is Qoigyijabu (Gyancain Norbu), while the Dalai Lama named Gedhun Choekyi Nyima on May 14, 1995. The latter vanished from public eye shortly after being named, aged six. Chinese authorities stated that Gedhun had been taken into protective custody and is now safe, but there is no information regarding from what, or from whom, he must be protected, where he is being held, or under what conditions. (Information – Wikipedia).

**Pavlova** A New Zealand food icon, named after the Russian ballerina Anna Pavlova. A large meringue cake covered in whipped cream and decorated with fresh fruit.

**Piu** (Tibetan) Monkey.

**Puja** (Sanskrit) Prayer, reverence, honour, worship.

**Rupee** (from Sanskrit raupya - silver) The currency of India. In late 2010 one hundred rupees was worth around US$2.25 or NZ$3.

**Samsara** (Sanskrit) The circle of life, death and rebirth. According to Buddhist belief, all beings have been suffering in Samsara for an unimaginable period, and they continue to do so until they attain Nirvana.

**Sangha** (Pali) In Buddhism, the Sangha means the monastic community of ordained monks and nuns, laymen and laywomen.

**Stupa** (Sanskrit) Mound-like structure containing sacred Buddhist relics. Tibetan - chorten. The Tibetan stupa is built on a square foundation symbolizing the earth, surmounted by a dome symbolizing water, and thirteen tapering steps of enlightenment which symbolize fire. These lead to a stylized parasol, the symbol of wind, topped by the twin symbol of the sun and moon, representing wisdom and method.

**Taking Refuge** To become a Buddhist you declare that you are taking refuge in the Buddha, the Dharma and the Sangha. i.e. that you have confidence that studying the Buddha's teachings and becoming part of the Buddhist community can help you deal with the sufferings of life, and avoid suffering in future lives.

**Tashi Delek** (Tibetan) Tibetan greeting, broadly translated as "May many good things come to you" or "Blessings and good luck."

**TESOL** Teachers of English to speakers of other languages.

**Thangka** (Tibetan) Painted picture of the Buddha or a mandala, surrounded by brocaded silk with a silk cover and mounted as a hanging. Originally designed to be carried from monastery to monastery and used as a teaching aid.

**TIPA** Tibetan Institute for the Performing Arts, located in McLeod Ganj. The institute preserves and promotes Tibet's unique tradition of performing arts including music, dance and opera.

**Trapa** (Tibetan) Monk, student.

**Tsampa** (Tibetan) Roasted barley meal made into a porridge. Traditional Tibetan staple food.

**Tuk tuk** Motorised rickshaw, moto, trishaw, auto rickshaw.

# Bibliography

Bansal, Sunita Pant. *Milarepa,* Delhi: Heritage Publishers, 2009

Central Tibetan Administration Planning Commission, *Demographic Survey of Tibetans in Exile - 2009.* Dharamshala: CTA, 2010

Chopra, Swati, *Dharamshala Diaries,* Delhi: Penguin Books, 2007

David-Neel, Alexandra, *My Journey to Lhasa,* Delhi: Time Books International, 1991

Friends of Tibet New Zealand, *Newsletter Vol XXII No.4,* Auckland: Friends of Tibet New Zealand, 2011

H.H. The Dalai Lama, Tenzin Gyatso, *How to Practise.* Isle of Man: Rider Books, 2003

Kyentse, Dzongsar Jamyang, *What Makes You Not a Buddhist.* Boston: Shambhala, 2007

Martin, Michele, *Music in the Sky. The life, art and teachings of the 17th Gyalwa Karmapa Ogyen Trinley Dorje,* Delhi: New Age Books, 2007

Pema, Jetsun, *Tibet: My Story.* Shaftesbury, Dorset: Element, 1997

Tenzing, Chime (Ed.), *50 Years in the Service of Tibetan Children in Exile. Golden Jubilee 1960 – 2010.* Dharmasala: Tibetan Children's Villages, 2010

## Internet sites consulted

**Wikipedia**
www.wikipedia.org
Diwali; Tibetan history; Chandigarh; Glossary definitions

**View on Buddhism**
www.viewonbuddhism.org
Buddhist definitions

## Some useful websites

**Dharamshala, including a contact for Sangye's Kitchen**
http://wikitravel.org/en/Dharamshala

**Friends of Tibet New Zealand**
www.friends-of-tibet.org.nz

**His Holiness the Dalai Lama**
www.dalailama.com

**Learning and Ideas for Tibet (LIT)**
http://learningandideasfortibet.org

**Salaam Baalak Trust**
www.salaambaalaktrust.com

**Tibet Charity**
www.tibetcharity.in

**Tibetan Children's Villages**
www.tcv.org.in

**Tibet Post news site**
www.thetibetpost.com

Printed in Great Britain
by Amazon